OFFICIAL
PREPARATION MATERIAL

Cambridge English

Joanna Kosta
Melanie Williams
Series Editor: Annette Capel

Prepare!

STUDENT'S BOOK
Level 1

Cambridge University Press
www.cambridge.org/elt

Cambridge English Language Assessment
www.cambridgeenglish.org

Information on this title: www.cambridge.org/9780521180436

© Cambridge University Press and UCLES 2015

First published 2015
20 19 18 17 16 15 14 13 12 11 10 9

Printed in Dubai by Oriental Press

A catalogue record for this publication is available from the British Library

ISBN 978-0-521-18043-6 Student's Book
ISBN 978-1-107-49715-3 Student's Book and Online Workbook
ISBN 978-0-521-18044-3 Workbook with Audio
ISBN 978-0-521-18045-0 Teacher's Book with DVD and Teacher's Resources Online
ISBN 978-0-521-18046-7 Class Audio CDs
ISBN 978-1-107-49714-6 Presentation Plus DVD-ROM

Contents

5

Welcome to *Prepare!*

Learn about the features in your new Student's Book

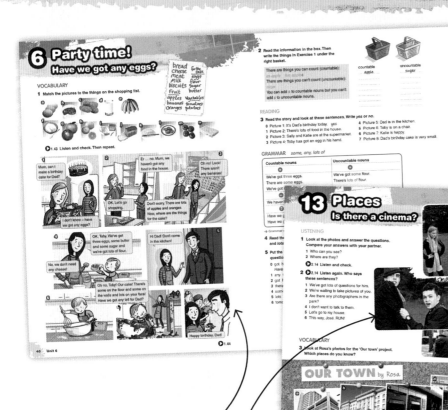

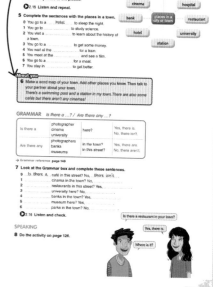

About you Talk about you and your life

Find new characters in the book

Video Watch interviews with teenagers like you

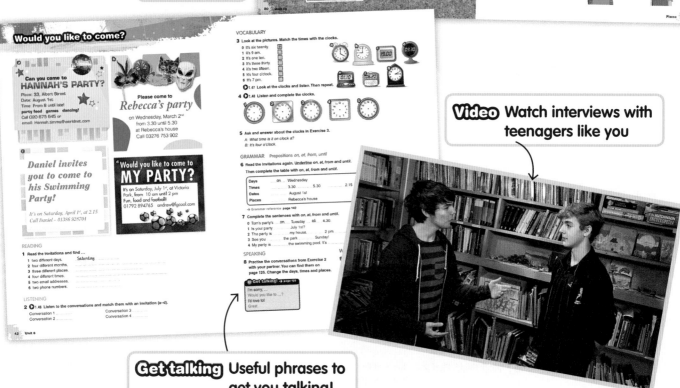

Get talking Useful phrases to get you talking!

Science
Robots

5 ▶1.59 Listen to some information about four robots. Match the robots to the photos.

| Replee Q1 | Asimo | Carp Robot | Spykee |

Robots

There are lots of different kinds of robots and they are very important in our world today. A lot of robots work for us. Some robots do dangerous jobs and other robots do difficult jobs or boring jobs. We need robots to do these things for us. But we can also have a lot of fun with robots.

6 ▶1.59 Listen again. One sentence for each robot is wrong. Find the wrong sentence and correct it.

Replee Q1 has got a beautiful face.
She can move her face and arms.
She can walk.

Carp robot is blue and silver.
It hasn't got a camera in its head.
It can give information about the water.

Asimo can't run.
Asimo can understand people's faces.
Asimo can open doors.

Spykee can take photos and make phone calls.
Spykee can't move.
Spykee can see and hear.

Project
Design and draw a robot. Think about these questions.
1 What can it do? (swim? walk? run? ... ?)
2 What has it got? (arms? legs? wheels? a camera? ... ?)
3 What is it for? (doing your homework? exploring planets? ... ?)
Work in a group. Tell each other about your robots.

My robot is called ...
It's got ...
It can ... and ...
It can't ... or ...

Project Work together to create something fun and expand your learning

Culture
Important places around the world

FAMOUS PLACES

1 Read the first paragraph and look at pictures A, B, C and D. Can you name these places? What countries are they in?

Every country has one or more very special places. These can be buildings, old cities, statues or even mountains. These places are very important to the people of that country. Sometimes the places are famous around the world too.

At Angkor, in Cambodia, there is an ancient stone city. Some of the buildings are about 2,000 years old. Angkor Wat is one of them. It is a very important temple in Cambodia. There is even a picture of it on the Cambodian flag. It has around a million visitors a year.

Machu Picchu is in Peru. It is an Inca city in the Andes mountains and it is 550 years old. There are many buildings there – temples, palaces, houses and gardens. There is also a pyramid. It is a very important place for learning about the Incas. It has about a million visitors a year.

The Taj Mahal is in the city of Agra, in India. It is a very famous and beautiful mausoleum, for a queen called Mumtaz Mahal. About three million people visit it every year. It is 360 years old.

Stonehenge is a very famous monument in the UK. It is an ancient stone circle. People began building it about 5,000 years ago, but even today, we are not sure how, or why it is there. Around 800,000 people a year visit Stonehenge from all over the world.

NEW WORDS
monument – an important building
pyramid – very old
temple – some people worship God in this building
mausoleum – this building is for the body of an important person
palace – a very important person lives in this building
statue –

2 Read the texts once to check your answers. Then read them again and complete the table.

	Name of place	Country	Age	Kind of place	Number of visitors	Interesting fact
A		India				
B			5,000 years old			
C	Stonehenge					People don't know why it is there.
D				city		

3 ▶2.20 Match the numbers with the words. Then listen, check and repeat.
a 100 — two hundred and fifty
b 250 — two million
c 1,000 — four hundred thousand
d 3,500 — three thousand five hundred
e 400,000 — a thousand
f 2,000,000 — a hundred

4 Practise saying these numbers with your partner.
440 1,200 650 4,000,000 3,000 6,800 300,000 1,500,000

5 Use the table to make sentences about the places. Your partner must say the name of the place.
This place is 360 years old. The Taj Mahal. Yes!

6 Look at the photographs E–H. Do you know these places?

7 Student A, turn to page 127. You have information about places E and F. Student B turn to page 129. You have information about places G and H. Ask and answer about the places.
A: What's place E called in English?
B: It is ...
A: Is it in Italy?
B: No, it isn't. It's in ...

Project
Work in pairs. Choose a famous place from your country, or another country. It can be a building, a statue, a mountain, a bridge, etc.
Write down:
• its name
• its age
• where it is
• what kind of place it is
• one or two interesting facts about it
Use books or the Internet to help you. Find a good photo.

Review Check your progress

Review 5
Units 17–20

LISTENING

1 ▶2.49 Gavin travelled to a lot of places this year. What was the weather like? Listen and draw a line.

January	February	March	April	May	June
wind	cold	rain	hot	warm	wind
rain	warm	hot	wind	rain	cold
warm	hot	cold	rain	wind	rain
hot	wind	warm	rain	cold	hot
cold	rain	wind	cold	hot	warm
warm	hot	wind	cold	snow	rain

VOCABULARY

2 Complete the sentences with a word from the box.
carry cat garden sea show train village

0 I love swimming in the ___ sea ___ on holiday.
1 Our ___ doesn't come with us on holiday. It goes to a kind of animal hotel.
2 Yesterday, I walked to the station to catch the ___.
3 You have some beautiful flowers in your ___.
4 Can you ___ me your new computer game?
5 A ___ is smaller than a town.
6 Shall I ___ your books for you?

3 Complete the words.
0 A person who doesn't have a lot of money is p___er.
1 In the summer, we sometimes go on a d___ o___ to a zoo.
2 I like to go by f___ train. It's fun and exciting.
3 Last year we travelled by car but it was very ___.
4 My brother likes playing on the b___ because he can't swim.
5 There are a lot of sheep on my uncle's f___.
6 I've got two t___ for the concert.

GRAMMAR

4 Make sentences with adjectives from the box. There is more than one answer.
big clean cold dirty easy exciting
expensive famous important
interesting new old young

0 apples / chocolate
Apples are nicer than chocolate.
1 your school bag / my school bag
2 José da Silva / our teacher
3 a visit to the zoo / a picnic in the country
4 writing English / speaking English
5 films / books
6 a flying boat / a plane

5 Complete the conversations with the correct preposition from the box.
for in on on until with with

1 A: Did you go to Sam's party ___ on Saturday evening?
B: Yes. I went ___ Paulina.
2 A: I waited for you ___ two o'clock! Where were you?
B: I was in my guitar lesson. I always have a guitar lesson ___ Monday.
3 A: Were you at this school last year?
B: No, I wasn't. I came here ___ September.
4 A: Where did you go on holiday last year?
B: I stayed ___ my friend in Spain ___ two weeks.

6 Read and complete the story. Use the past simple.
Bobby ⁰ lived (live) in a flat in New York. Every day he ¹ ___ (travel) to school by bus. He ² ___ (not walk) to school because the school ³ ___ (be) a long way from his house. One day, Bobby ⁴ ___ (want) to get to school before his friends. He ⁵ ___ (start) to walk because it ⁶ ___ (be) too early for the bus. He ⁷ ___ (walk) and ⁸ ___ (walk) for an hour. Where ⁹ ___ (be) the school? He ¹⁰ ___ (ask) a man in a shop. 'Do you know where Main Street School is?' 'Yes, the man ¹¹ ___ (say). 'It's only five minutes from here.' When Bobby ¹² ___ (arrive) at school he ¹³ ___ (be) very happy because he ¹⁴ ___ (not be) late for class.

SPEAKING

7 Do an interview with an explorer. Write questions with be in the past and present. Ask and answer with your partner.
Where ...
What kind of clothes/food ...
How long/cold ...
Why ...
Who ...

READING

8 A haiku is a short poem with three lines. Haikus are often about the weather. Read the haikus and match each one to a picture.

Snow
on the cold glass,
but inside it's warm.

Summer night –
in bed but not sleeping,
listening to the rain.

Long summer days,
there's no school for months.
Why am I sad?

The beach in winter,
cold wind in my face,
water in my shoes.

First snow of winter,
all the trees
have new clothes.

WRITING

9 Choose a picture and write your own haiku.

Find ...

in your Student's Book

In the classroom
What's your name?

THE ALPHABET

1 ▶1.02 Listen and repeat the letters.

Aa Bb Cc Dd Ee Ff Gg Hh Ii
Jj Kk Ll Mm Nn Oo Pp Qq Rr
Ss Tt Uu Vv Ww Xx Yy Zz

2 ▶1.03 Listen and write the names.

 a  b  c  d  e  f  g

3 ▶1.04 Listen and repeat. Then ask and answer with your partner.

What's your name?

Tim.

How do you spell it?

T-I-M.

NUMBERS

4 ▶1.05 Listen and repeat the numbers.

1 one 2 two 3 three 4 four 5 five 6 six 7 seven 8 eight 9 nine 10 ten 11 eleven
12 twelve 13 thirteen 14 fourteen 15 fifteen 16 sixteen 17 seventeen 18 eighteen 19 nineteen 20 twenty

5 How many candles? Write the number in words.

nine

6 ▶1.06 Look at the cakes in Exercise 5. Listen and match the people with the cakes. Write a letter in the box.

1 Nat: cake [d]
2 Penny: cake [ ]
3 Jack: cake [ ]
4 Tim: cake [ ]
5 Anna: cake [ ]
6 Lara: cake [ ]

7 Listen to your teacher. Write four numbers. Then play a game.

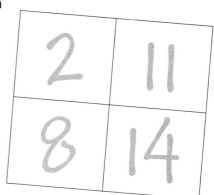

DAYS

8 ▶1.07 Listen and repeat. Then write the days.

Wednesday   Saturday   Tuesday   *Friday*

January

Monday	....	....	Thursday	....	....	Sunday
1	2	3	4	5	6	7
8	9	10	11	12	13	14

9 ▶1.08 Listen and repeat. Then practise with your partner.

Tuesday, Wednesday …

… Thursday!

SPEAKING

10 Write three questions. Then walk around the class and ask and answer.

What	do you spell it?
How	is your name?
	old are you?

This pen is red

a apple   b rubber   c orange

g picture   h ruler   i pen

k pencil   l pencil case

d board   e teacher

f book

j desk

m boy   n girl

THE CLASSROOM

1 ▶ 1.09 Listen and repeat.

2 Point and say the words.

a desk

a board

three pictures

a / an

a ruler   a book   an apple   an orange
two rulers   three books   four apples

COLOURS

3 Match the colours with the words.

| black | blue | brown | green | grey |
| orange | red | white | yellow |

1   orange

▶ 1.10 Listen and check. Then repeat.

1 2 3 4 5

6 7 8 9

4 Say the colour, not the word!

0 black *yellow*

1 blue

2 brown

3 green

4 grey

5 orange

6 red

7 white

8 yellow

5 Write sentences.

The pencil is yellow.

 0

 1

  2

3

4

5

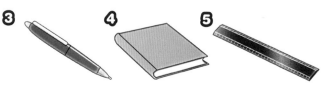

6 **Read the sentences. Match them to the pictures.**

1 This pencil is red.   c
2 These pencils are orange.
3 That book is green.
4 Those books are blue.

7 **Complete the sentences with *this, that, these, those* and a colour word.**

0 .....This..... desk is .....brown...... .

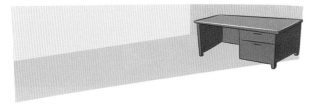

1 .... desk is ....

2 .... pens are ....

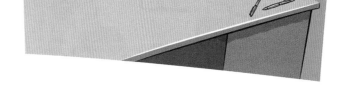

3 .... pens are ....

4 .... ruler is ....

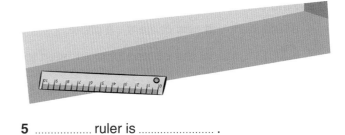

5 .... ruler is ....

8 **Ask and answer about things in your classroom.**

A: *What colour are these books?*
B: *Blue.*

A: *What colour is that desk?*
B: *Brown.*

9 ▶1.11 **Listen and repeat.**

January   February   March   April   May   June

July   August   September   October   November   December

10 ▶1.12 **Listen and repeat. Then walk around the class. Ask and answer the question.**

When's your birthday?

In November.

11 **Complete the chart for the class.**

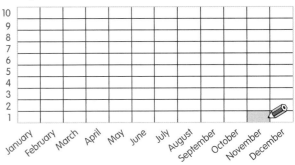

1 All about me
New friends

Hi. I'm Joelle.

Hi, Joelle. My name's Rosa. And this is Paolo.

Hello, Joelle.

Look, Rosa! Her phone's red …

… and his phone's red!

See you later.

See you Saturday.

Goodbye, Joelle. Bye, Rosa.

LISTENING AND VOCABULARY

1 Find these things in the photos.

a red phone   a new camera   a photo

2 ▶1.13 Look at the photos again. Listen to the conversation and find Rosa, Joelle and Paolo.

3 ▶1.13 Read. Then listen again and tick (✔).

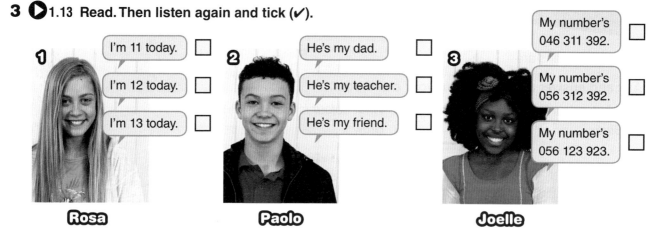

1
I'm 11 today. ☐
I'm 12 today. ☐
I'm 13 today. ☐

Rosa

2
He's my dad. ☐
He's my teacher. ☐
He's my friend. ☐

Paolo

3
My number's 046 311 392. ☐
My number's 056 312 392. ☐
My number's 056 123 923. ☐

Joelle

4 ▶1.14 Listen and repeat.

Clara: Hi. I'm Clara.
Nick: Hi, Clara. My name's Nick. And this is Maya.
Maya: Hello, Clara.
…
Clara: See you later.
Nick: Yes. See you Monday.
Maya: Goodbye, Nick. Bye, Clara.

5 Practise in groups of three. Use your names.

EP Get talking!

Hi.
Hello.
Goodbye.
Bye.
See you later.
See you Saturday.

GRAMMAR Determiners

This is my camera.
What's your phone number?
    Her phone's red.
And his phone's red.

6 Complete the sentences.

0 My... name's Tom... .

1 .... name's Jo.

2 .... name's
....

3 .... name's
....

About you
8 Draw a picture of you.
Talk to your partner about it.
My name's Monika.
I'm 11.
This is my camera.
It's yellow.

be singular ➕

I'm Joelle.	(I am)
You're funny!	(You are)
She's my teacher.	(She is)
He's my dad.	(He is)
It's new.	(It is)

→ Grammar reference page 137

7 Complete the sentences.

0 I'm..... Nora.

1 It .... green.

2 She .... my friend.

3 He .... my teacher.

4 I .... Ben.

5 And you .... a student.

SPEAKING

**9 Play the game in groups of four. Put your
pictures on the table. Take turns to speak.**

Your name's Jason. You're 11.
Your book is green.

Where are you from?

Where are you from?

READING AND VOCABULARY

1 Read about people from different countries.

Tell us about you.

How old are you?   What's your name?   Where are you from?

Hi. My name's Yannis and I'm 14. I'm Greek.

Hi. I'm Alejandro and I'm 15. I'm from Mexico.

Hi. I'm Timur and I'm 13. I'm Turkish.

Hello. We're Luisa and Ana. We're 11 and we're twins! We're from Brazil.

Hi. My name's Li Ying and I'm Chinese. I'm 12.

Hello. I'm from Russia. I'm 16 and my name's Irina.

2 Read again and complete the table.

Country	Nationality
1 Greece	Greek
2 Turkey	
3	Mexican
4	Brazilian
5	Russian
6 China	

About you

3 Write about you.
- your name
- your age
- your country
- your nationality

My name's Laura and I'm 13 years old. I'm from Colombia. I'm Colombian.
Find your country on the map.

Find the countries on the map. Write the number.

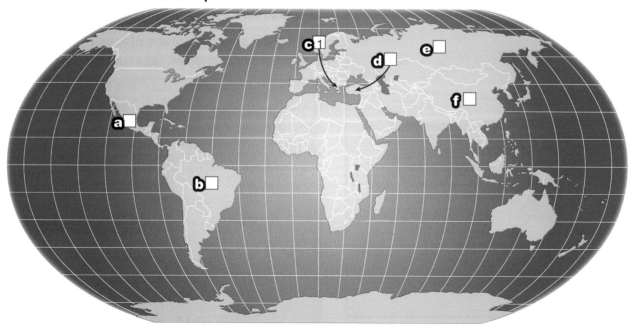

PRONUNCIATION *from*

4 1.15 **Listen and repeat.**

A: *Where are you from?*
B: *I'm from China.*

Then ask and answer with your partner.

VOCABULARY

5 ▶1.16 **Listen and complete the chant.**

Hi! Hello! Where are you from?
What's your nationality?

I'm Greek.

She's Greek!
She isn't (0) *Chinese* .
She's Greek!
Hi! Hello! Where are you from?
What's your nationality?

I'm German.

He's German!
He isn't (1) ....
He's German!
Hi! Hello! Where are you from?
What's your nationality?

We're Brazilian.

They're Brazilian.
They aren't (2) ....
They're Brazilian!
Hi! Hello! Where are you from?
What's your nationality?

We're Russian.

You're Russian.
You aren't (3) ....
You're Russian!

GRAMMAR   *be* plural ➕

We're	(We are)	
You're	(You are)	Russian.
They're	(They are)	from Russia.

be singular and plural ➖

I	'm not	(I am not)	
You	aren't	(You are not)	
He	isn't	(He is not)	
She	isn't	(She is not)	Greek.
We	aren't	(We are not)	
You	aren't	(You are not)	
They	aren't	(They are not)	

→ Grammar reference **page 137**

6 ▶1.16 **Listen again and say the chant.**

7 **Complete columns A and B in the table with 10 countries.**

	A –	B +	
0	France	Germany	He ...*isn't*... from ...*France*...... . ...*He's*... from ...*Germany*.... .
0	Russia	Greece	They ...*aren't*..... ...*Russian*.. . ...*They're*.... ...*Greek*...... .
1	....	....	We .... from .... from ....
2	....	....	They ....
3	....	....	You .... from .... from ....
4	....	....	She ....
5	....	....	I .... from .... from ....

Write your country here.

8 **Look at the examples in the table and complete the sentences.**

WRITING

9 **Write a chant.**

2 Families
Who's this?

Hello. My name's Sally. This is my family – my husband and my three children. We're from Manchester.

Hi. I'm Jason. This is my wife. Her name's Sally. These are our two sons. Their names are Nat and Toby. Our daughter's name is Katie.

Hello. I'm Nat and I'm 14. My sister's name is Katie. These are my parents and this is my baby brother. He's called Toby. Ow, Toby, stop!

Hi. My name's Katie. I'm 11 and my brother Nat is 14. Our baby brother is two. This is my mother and father. Their names are Sally and Jason but we call them Mum and Dad!

▶1.17

READING AND VOCABULARY

1 Read and complete the table.

	Katie	Sally and Jason	Nat and Toby	Toby	Katie and Nat
mum and dad		✔			
brother and sister					
parents					
daughter					
husband and wife					
brothers					
sons					
children					
mother and father					

2 ▶1.18 Listen to the family words and repeat them.

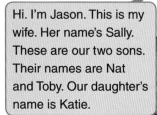

PRONUNCIATION *and*

3 ▶1.19 **Listen and repeat.**

1 Mum and Dad
2 brother and sister
3 husband and wife
4 family and friends
5 mother and father
6 French and German

GRAMMAR *their, our* and *'s*

Nat is Katie's brother.	Nat is her brother.
Katie is Nat's sister.	Katie is his sister.
Katie is Jason and Sally's daughter.	Katie is their daughter.

→ Grammar reference **page 138**

4 Complete the sentences about the family.

0 Toby is Jason's ....son........ .
1 Jason is Nat's ....
2 Katie is Sally's ....
3 Sally is Jason's ....
4 Jason and Sally are Katie's ....
5 Nat, Katie and Toby are Jason and Sally's
....

5 Look at the picture of the family for two minutes. Then close the book and talk about the family with your partner.

Nat is Sally's son.

Yes!

Toby is Katie's sister.

No, he's Katie's brother.

6 Read about the family on page 18 again. <u>Underline</u> examples of *their* and *our*.

7 Complete the sentences with *their* or *our*.

❶

This is .... mother.

❷

These are my brothers. ....
names are Nat and Toby.

❸

.... children are 14, 11 and 2.
.... names are Nat, Katie and Toby.

About you

8 Draw your family. Ask and answer with your partner.
A: Who's this?
B: That's my sister. She's called Pia. She's 10.

Are you bored?

VOCABULARY

1 Look at the pictures and complete the sentences.

| bored clever funny happy hot |
| hungry nice sad tired |

0 I'm ......*bored*...... .

1 I'm ....   **2** I'm ....   **3** I'm ....   **4** I'm ....

5 He's ....   **6** You're ....   **7** They're ....   **8** She's ....

▶ 1.20 Listen and check. Then repeat the sentences.

LISTENING

2 ▶ 1.21 Look at the picture story. Listen and number the pictures.

3 ▶ 1.21 Listen again. Write *yes* or *no*.

1 Bella is Spanish.   *no*   **4** The film is funny.

2 Bella is hungry.   **5** Sue and Bella are bored.

3 Sue is hot.   **6** Bella is happy.

GRAMMAR *be* ❓ and short answers

4 Match the *Yes / No* questions with the short answers.

Yes / No questions	Short answers	*Wh-* questions	Remember
Are you Spanish?	No, we aren't.	Where are you from?	You are Spanish.
Are you hungry?	No, it isn't.	How old are you?	
Is she hot?	Yes, she is.		Are you Spanish?
Is the film funny?	No, they aren't.		
Are you bored?	Yes, I am.		
Are they tired?	No, I'm not.		

→ Grammar reference **page 138**

5 Complete the conversations.

    0 ....*Are*........ your friends hot?
       No, they ......*aren't*...... . They're fine!
    1 .... you tired?
       No, we ....
    2 .... your parents French?
       Yes, they ....
    3 .... Tom sad?
       No, he .... He's bored.
    4 .... you bored?
       No, I .... I'm tired.
    5 .... your teacher clever?
       Yes, she ....
    6 .... your brothers hungry?
       No, they ....

6 Work in pairs. Practise the conversations in Exercise 5.

About you

7 Write short answers to these questions. Then ask and answer with your partner.
- Are you bored today?
- Is your teacher nice?
- Is the classroom hot today?
- Are your parents funny?
- Are you Brazilian?
- Is your friend sad today?

SPEAKING

8 Complete the information about you.

Home	**Profile**	Friends

Info | Photos | +

Me

Name
Age
Nationality
Today I'm   ☐ happy   ☐ sad
            ☐ bored   ☐ hot
            ☐ angry

9 Ask and answer with your partner about the information in Exercise 8.

What's your name?

Tomas.

WRITING

10 Write about your partner.

My partner's name is ....
He is .... years old.
He is ....
Today he is ....

Culture
The United Kingdom

Loch Ness

The Shambles, York

The Giant's Causeway

Caernarfon Castle

Big Ben, London

● CAPITAL CITY

The three countries in Great Britain are England, Scotland and Wales.
The United Kingdom is England, Scotland, Wales and Northern Ireland.

National flowers

England
a rose

Scotland
a thistle

Wales
a daffodil

Northern Ireland
a shamrock

Brighton pier

The name of the money in the UK is
pounds £ and pence p
£2.00 two pounds
10p ten pence

Popular sports in the UK are football and rugby.
Cricket is popular in England and Wales.

1 Match the countries and nationalities.

Country	Nationality
England	Welsh
Scotland	Irish
Wales	British
Ireland	Scottish
Britain	English

▶ 1.22 Listen, check and repeat.

2 Look at the map and the pictures and read the information. Write the name of the country.

1 Big Ben is in ....
2 Loch Ness is in ....
3 Caernarfon Castle is in ....
4 Cricket is popular in ....
5 The Giant's Causeway is in ....

3 Answer the questions.

1 What is the national flower of Scotland?
2 What is the name of the money in the UK?

4 Write the capital cities.

1 Scotland ....
2 England ....
3 Wales ....
4 Northern Ireland ....

5 Write the colours of the flags.

1 English flag:
.... and ....

2 Scottish flag:
.... and ....

3 Welsh flag:
.... , ... and
....

4 British flag:
.... , ... and
....

6 ▶ 1.23 Listen and complete the table.

	1	2	3
Name			
Nationality			
Dad's nationality			
Mum's nationality			

Project

Make a poster about your country.
On your poster, put:
- a map of your country
- a picture of your flag
- your national flower
- the names of important cities
- names and pictures of important places
- information about your country's favourite sports
- information about your country's money

3 My home
Paolo's house

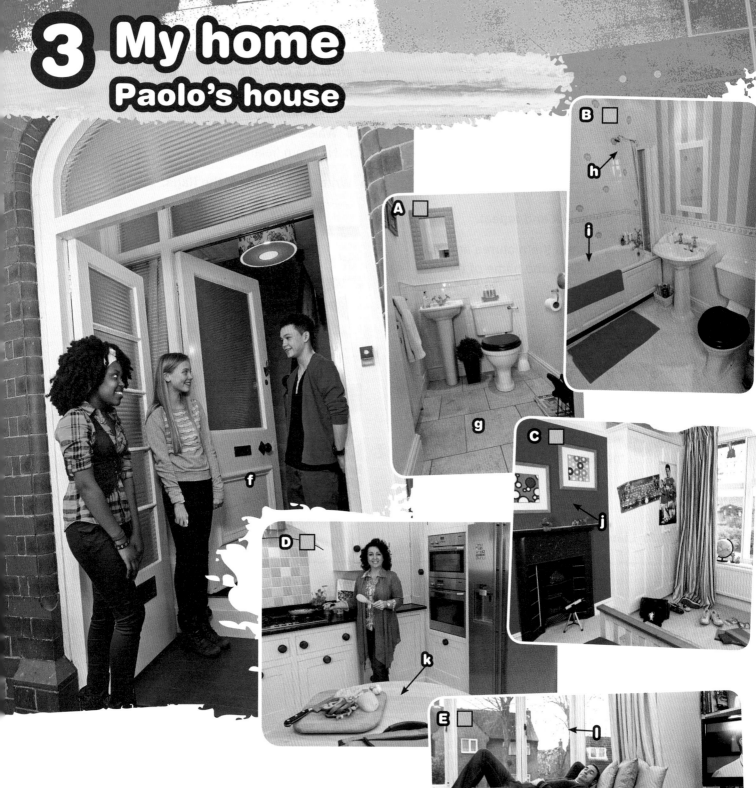

VOCABULARY

1 Match the rooms A–E in the photos to the words in the box.

> bathroom   bedroom   kitchen   living room   toilet

2 Match the things f–l to the words in the box.

> bath   door   floor   shower   table   wall   window

▶1.24 **Listen and check. Then repeat the words.**

LISTENING

3 ▶1.25 **Joelle and Rosa are at Paolo's house. Listen and number the rooms as you hear them.**

GRAMMAR *there is / there are*   *in/on*

There's (There is)	There are	in/on
There's a table in the kitchen.	There are three rooms.	Dad's in the living room.
There's a toilet here.	There are three bedrooms.	The bags are on the table.
There's a shower and a bath.	There are two windows.	

→ Grammar reference **page 139**

4 **Look at the examples in the table. Complete the sentences with *is/are* and *in/on*.**

1 There .... one camera
.... the box.

2 There .... three cameras
.... the box.

5 ▶1.26 **Look at the photos on page 24 again and listen to the sentences. Write Y (*yes*) or N (*no*).**

0	...Y...	2	....	4	....
1	....	3	....	5	....

▶1.26 **Listen again and repeat.**

6 **Complete the sentences with *There's* or *There are*. Then match them with the pictures.**

0 ..*There are*.. two girls in the pink bedroom.
  Molly's house

1 .... four people in the kitchen.

2 .... a shower in the bathroom.

3 .... a table in the kitchen.

4 .... two windows in the living room.

5 .... six books on the floor in the
blue bedroom.

6 .... five pictures on the walls in
the living room.

7 .... a baby in the bath.

8 .... a boy in the kitchen.

About you

7 Tell your partner five things about
your home.
I live in a flat. There are six rooms.

WRITING

8 **Write about your partner's home.**

*Luigi's home is a flat. There are two
toilets and …*

I live in a house.

Molly

I live in a flat.

Jay

In my room

VOCABULARY

1 ▶ 1.27 Listen and repeat.
Find the things in the bedrooms.

3 clock

4 computer

5 computer games

6 clothes

2 chair

1 bed

7 DVDs

8 guitar

9 radio

10 pet fish

11 television (TV)

READING

2 Read the magazine article. Match the people with the rooms.

Luisa

This is my room. It's got blue walls and a light brown floor. There's a bed and a chair in here. I've got lots of clothes. They're all on the bed and the floor. I've also got a TV and about ten DVDs. My favourite film is *School of Rock*!

Jozef

This is my room. I've got a computer and I've got lots of computer games. My brothers have got a computer in their room too. I've also got a guitar and a radio in here. I've got lots of pictures of my favourite bands on the walls.

Agata

This is my room and my sister's. There are two beds and a chair. There's a clock on the wall. We've got lots of books. My sister's got two pet fish, called Nemo and Dory. They've got a little house and lots of plants in their aquarium!

3 Complete the sentences. Compare your answers with your partner.

My favourite band is

....

My favourite film is

....

My favourite thing is

....

My favourite person is

....

My favourite book is

....

GRAMMAR   *have got* ➕

| I / you / we / they | 've got (have got) |
| he / she / it | 's got (has got) |

→ Grammar reference **page 139**

4 Read the article in Exercise 2 again. <u>Underline</u> all the examples of *'ve got, 's got* and *have got*.

5 Complete the sentences from the article.

0 I ....*'ve got*.... a computer.
1 My sister .... two pet fish.
2 It .... blue walls.
3 We .... lots of books.
4 They .... a little house.
5 My brothers .... a computer too.
6 I .... lots of clothes.

6 Complete the sentences with *'ve got, 's got* and *have got*.

1 My Dad .... a nice mobile phone.
2 My parents .... a television in their bedroom.
3 I .... two brothers and a sister.
4 Your brother .... lots of friends.
5 Rosa and David .... new cameras.
6 You .... my dictionary!

PRONUNCIATION   Lists

7 ▶1.28 **Listen and repeat.**

1 I've got a chair, a table and a desk.
2 I've got a guitar, a radio and a TV.
3 My brother's got a camera, a phone and a computer.
4 In our flat, there's a kitchen, a living room and two bedrooms.
5 The teacher's got a book, a pen, a ruler and a dictionary.

8 Play in groups.

> In our bedroom, we've got a bed.

> In our bedroom, we've got a bed and a chair.

> In our bedroom, we've got a bed, a chair and a dictionary.

WRITING

9 Read the sentences about Sara's room. <u>Underline</u> examples of *also*.

I've got a bed and a chair in my room. I've also got a desk. On my desk, I've got a book and two pens. I've also got a computer.

10 Take a photo of your room or draw it. Write about it. Use *also* in one or two of your sentences.

4 My things
Oh no! The chocolate!

Nat's bag

Katie's bag

VOCABULARY

1 Look at the pictures. Say the names of the things you know.

▶ 1.29 Listen and check. Then repeat.

READING

2 Read the story and complete the sentence.

.... has got the chocolate.

3 Read the story again. Match the things with Katie and Nat's bags. Write K (*Katie*) or N (*Nat*) in the boxes.

a drink ☐
a coat ☐
a ball ☐
a hat ☐
a banana ☐
a football ☐
a phone ☐
keys ☐

▶ 1.31 Listen and check.

▶ 1.30

4 Write sentences about the things in your bag.

I've got four books, a phone, a drink and a computer game.

PRONUNCIATION   Syllables •

5 ▶1.32 **Listen and write the words in the table.**

• friend	•• guitar	••• Saturday

GRAMMAR   *have got* ⊖

He	hasn't got	the chocolate.
She	hasn't got	the chocolate.
We	haven't got	the chocolate.
They	haven't got	the chocolate.
You	haven't got	the chocolate.
I	haven't got	the chocolate.

Toby!!!

→ **Grammar reference** **page 140**

6 ▶1.33 **Listen to the sentences.**
<u>Underline</u> **the words you hear.**

0 *I haven't got / I've got* my things.
1 *He hasn't got / He's got* a coat.
2 *You've got / You haven't got* a sister.
3 *They haven't got / They've got* a TV in the kitchen.
4 *She's got / She hasn't got* a new bag.
5 *I haven't got / I've got* my drink.
6 *We've got / We haven't got* a clock in the classroom.

7 **Complete the sentences.**

0 My little sister *hasn't got* a hat.
   She *'s got* a coat.

1 My little brother .... a football.
   He .... a guitar.

2 We .... a bath in our house.
   We .... a shower.

3 They .... a television.
   They .... a pet fish.

4 My sister .... a banana.
   She .... some chocolate.

5 You .... some keys.
   You .... a phone.

6 I .... a drink on my table.
   I .... a book.

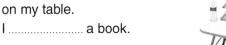

SPEAKING

8 **Look at the picture on page 124 for one minute. Then close your book. What can you remember? Tell your partner.**

Nat hasn't got a computer. I think he's got a phone.

I think Katie's got a banana. Yes, look! She's got a banana.

Have you got my red bag?

VOCABULARY adjectives

1 Look at the picture and find these things.

a long yellow ruler

a big red bag

a new green coat

a dark red coat

a black and white hat

a dirty red and yellow football

> long   short   dirty   clean   big   small
> new   old   dark blue   light blue

2 Look at the picture and find these things.

a short, red ruler

a small, brown bag

an old, grey coat

a light grey coat

a clean, black and white football

3 ▶1.34 Listen and number the sentences.

It's a dirty, dark brown bag. ☐

It's a clean, light blue bag. ☐

It's a long, new ruler. ☐

It's a short, red ruler. ☐ 1

It's a dark blue coat. ☐

It's an old, grey coat. ☐

▶1.34 Listen again and repeat.

4 Talk about the picture in Exercise 1 with your partner.

A: There are four bags in the picture. This bag is light brown and it's small and dirty.

B: There's one black and white hat. Look, here it is.

About you

5 Write about your things. Use the picture in Exercise 1 to help you.

I've got a new school bag. It's dark green and yellow. It's big. I've also got a new coat. It's …

LISTENING

6 ▶1.35 **Listen and tick (✔) the things that Emma hasn't got.**

She hasn't got   her coat. ☐
her pencil. ☐
her bag. ☐
her ruler. ✔
her football things. ☐
her hat. ☐

7 ▶1.35 **Look at the picture in Exercise 1 and listen again. Find Emma's things.**

GRAMMAR   *have got* ❓

Have I got my books?

Have you got my keys?

Has he got my dictionary?

Have we got a new English book?

Has she got my phone?

Have they got my bag?

Has it got my football things inside?

Yes, it has!

Short answers
Yes, I have. / No, I haven't.
Yes, you have. / No, you haven't.
Yes, he/she/it has. / No, he/she/it hasn't.
Yes, we have. / No, we haven't.
Yes, they have. / No, they haven't.

→ Grammar reference **page 140**

8 **Read the Grammar box. Complete the sentences.**

0 **A:** ....Has.... he got a pet fish?
B: No, he .....hasn't..... .

1 **A:** .... Emma got her bag?
B: No, she ....

2 **A:** .... Katie and Nat got Toby's ball?
B: Yes, they ....

3 **A:** .... I got your phone?
B: Yes, you ....

4 **A:** .... you got your glasses?
B: No, I ....

5 **A:** .... your bag got my football things inside?
B: Yes, it ....

▶1.36 **Listen and check.**

9 **Ask and answer with your partner.**

A: Have you got a clock on your kitchen wall?
B: Yes, I have.

… a clock on your kitchen wall?
… a shower in your house?
… your keys in your bag?
… a chair in your bedroom?
… your English books on your desk?
… photos on your bedroom wall?

SPEAKING

10 **What have you got at school? Talk about the things in the box with your partner.**

notebook   apple   pencil case   phone   hat
ruler   keys   glasses   a drink   pet fish

What things have you got at school?

I've got an apple and I've got my phone. It's new and it's dark blue and black. I haven't got my hat. I've got my dark green notebook. I've got my white ruler but I haven't got my pet fish!

Geography
People and continents

Hello, my name's Sanjit and I'm ten. This is my family. We're Indian. My sister is called Harita and she's fourteen. My mum's name is Naisha and my dad's name is Lalit. In my country it's hot in winter and very hot in summer.

Hi, I'm Eduardo and I'm thirteen years old. I'm with my mum and dad and my sister in the photo. We're Colombian. My mum and dad are called Maria and Javier. My sister's name is Andrea and she's eight. In my country it's warm in the summer and warm in the winter.

Hi, my name's Mandisa and I'm eleven. This is a photo of me and my family. We're South African. My sister's name is Puleng. We're twins. My mum and dad are called Kefilwe and Baruti. In my country it's warm and dry in summer and cool and wet in winter.

Hi, I'm Maya and I'm fourteen. This is a photo of my family in the winter. We're Canadian. I haven't got brothers or sisters. I'm an only child. My mom and dad are called Elizabeth and Adam. In my country it's very cold in the winter and warm in the summer.

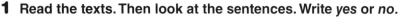

1 Read the texts. Then look at the sentences. Write _yes_ or _no_.

Sanjit
0 Sanjit is Indian. yes
1 He's 14.
2 His mum is called Harita.
3 In his country it's hot in winter.

Eduardo
1 Eduardo is 13.
2 He's South African.
3 His sister's called Andrea.
4 In his country, it's hot in the summer.

Mandisa
1 Mandisa is Colombian.
2 She's got one brother.
3 Her sister is called Kefilwe.
4 Her sister is 11.

Maya
1 Maya is 14.
2 She's Canadian.
3 Her sister's name is Elizabeth.
4 In her country it isn't cold in winter.

2 Complete the sentences with the name of the country.

1 Sanjit is from ....

2 Eduardo is from ....

3 Mandisa is from ....

4 Maya is from ....

3 Find the countries from Exercise 2 on the map below.

4 Match the pictures with the weather words.

1 cold
2 cool
3 hot
4 warm
5 wet
6 dry

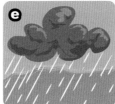

5 Write the names of the countries in Exercise 2. Which country is

1 warm in summer and cool in winter? ....

2 warm in summer and winter? ....

3 very cold in winter? ....

4 hot in summer and in winter? ....

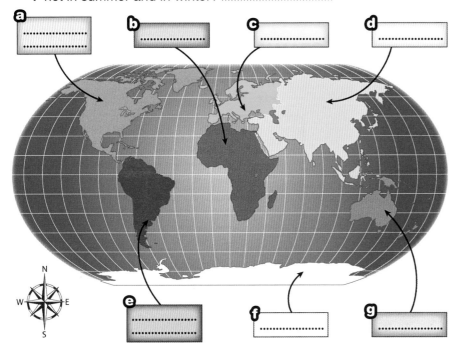

6 Find the seven continents on the map. Then find the English names for the seven continents in your dictionary or on the internet. Write the names of the continents in the boxes.

7 Look at the map. Ask and answer about countries and continents.

A: *Where's Greece?*

B: *It's in Europe.*

B: *What's a country in Asia?*

A: *China.*

Project

Find a photo of your family. Write about your family and your country.

Hi, my name's Liuba and I'm eleven. This is a photo of me and my family. We're Russian.

Review 1
Units 1–4

VOCABULARY

1 Complete the puzzle. There's a word in the purple spaces. What is it?

 1
 2
 3
 4

 5
 6
 7
 8
 9

2 Put the letters in the right order to make family words.

0 tressi *sister*

1 bhsunda
2 uhtdraeg
3 fwei
4 nos
5 add
6 rtnepas

7 torbrhe
8 drnhicle
9 hrtemo
10 frheta
11 mmu
12 ybba

3 Match the adjectives with the people. Close your book and ask and answer with a partner.

> bored clever funny happy hot hungry
> sad tired

A: Is Joe funny?
B: Yes, he is.

GRAMMAR

4 Complete the sentences with the words in the box.

> They're I'm are It's He's She's We're
> ~~My~~ is (x 2) His Her

Hi! ¹ ......My...... name's Joelle. ² .... twelve.
These ³ .... my new friends. ⁴ ....
really nice!
This ⁵ .... Paolo. ⁶ .... thirteen.
⁷ .... Dad's Italian.
This ⁸ .... Rosa. ⁹ .... thirteen.
¹⁰ .... camera's new!
¹¹ .... in a photo club. ¹² .... fun!

5 Look at the picture and complete the sentences.

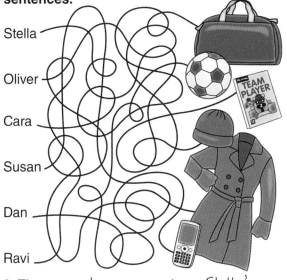

Stella
Oliver
Cara
Susan
Dan
Ravi

0 The .....*computer game*..... is ....*Stella's*........ .
1 The .... is ....
2 The .... is ....
3 The .... is ....
4 The .... is ....
5 The .... is ....

6 Play this game.

Write down six things in your bag.

Ask and answer with your partner.

You get one point when your partner says *Yes, I have.*

Count your points. Who is the winner?

Have you got a phone?

Yes, I have.

Have you got a ruler?

No, I haven't.

READING

7 Read about Anna's home. Are the sentences right (✔) or wrong (✗)?

My name's Anna and I live in a flat with my mum and dad. We've got five rooms – a kitchen, a living room, a bathroom and two bedrooms. In the kitchen there's a small table with five chairs. There's also a TV and a radio. In the living room there's a desk and a computer. There are three pictures on the walls. In the bathroom there's a shower. We haven't got a bath. My favourite room is my bedroom. I've got a desk, a chair and a small table in here. On the desk there are my books and photos of my friends. My guitar is on the chair.

0 There are six rooms in the flat. ✗
1 There's a table in the kitchen.
2 There's a computer in the kitchen.
3 There are four pictures in the living room.
4 There's a bath in the bathroom.
5 There's a big table in Anna's bedroom.
6 There are photos on Anna's desk.
7 There's a guitar in Anna's bedroom.

WRITING

8 Write these sentences with capital letters and full stops.

0 my name's gabby and i'm 14
   My name's Gabby and I'm 14.
1 my mum's from brazil and my dad's from mexico
2 my friend ling is chinese
3 they aren't from poland
4 he isn't french, he's russian
5 my teacher's called mr brown
6 i'm from germany

5 Yes, we can!
What can you do?

VOCABULARY

1 Look at pictures a–f in the table. Complete Line 1 with words from the box.

> paint a picture   play the guitar   ~~ride a horse~~
> sing   speak Italian   swim underwater

	a	**b**	**c**	**d**	**e**	**f**
Line 1 →	ride a horse					
Joelle can	✔					
Rosa can						
Paolo can						

▶1.37 Listen and check. Then repeat.

LISTENING

2 ▶1.38 Look at the photo at the top of the page and listen. Write *yes* or *no*.

0 The friends are in the park.   yes
1 Next week's photo club project is 'Sport'.
2 Rosa's camera is old.
3 The new boy is called José.
4 He's got a very nice camera.

3 ▶1.38 Read the Grammar box. Then listen again. What can Joelle, Rosa and Paolo do? Tick (✔) the table in Exercise 1.

GRAMMAR   *can / can't*

➕
I / you / he / she / it / we / they can swim.

➖
I / you / he / she / it / we / they can't (can not) swim.

❓
What can you do?
Short answers
Can you swim?   Yes, I can.   No, I can't.

→ Grammar reference **page 141**

4 Complete the sentences with *can* or *can't*.

0 Joelle ....*can*.... ride a horse.
1 Rosa .... swim underwater.
2 Paolo .... sing or ride a horse.
3 .... Paolo paint a picture?
No, he ....
4 .... Paolo speak Italian?
Yes, he ....

PRONUNCIATION   *can / can't*

5 ▶ 1.39 **Listen and repeat.**

What can you do?
Can you ride a horse?

No, I can't.

Can you play the guitar?

No, I can't.

Well, can you take photos?

Yes, I can. And I
can speak Italian.

Oh good!

About you

6 Write short answers to these questions. Then
ask and answer with your partner.
- Can you use a dictionary?
- Can you take good photographs?
- Can you draw a horse?
- Can your mother sing?
- Can you swim 25 metres?
- Can your teacher remember your name?

7 ▶ 1.40 **Listen and <u>underline</u> the word
you hear.**

0 I <u>can</u> / *can't* take good photos.
1 We *can* / *can't* see the TV.
2 I *can* / *can't* remember her name.
3 My sister *can* / *can't* play the guitar.
4 *Can* / *Can't* your little brother read?
5 My mother *can* / *can't* speak Chinese.

SPEAKING

8 What can you do? Put a ✔ (yes) or a ✗ (no) in
the *Me* column.

9 Ask and answer with your partner. Use
can and *can't*. Complete the table for your
partner.

	Me	My partner
play the guitar		
ride a horse		
swim underwater		
paint a picture		
sing		
speak Italian / French / Chinese		
take photos		

Can you play
the guitar?

No, I can't.

WRITING

10 Read the sentences in the table. Then
write three sentences about you and three
sentences about your partner. Use *and, but*
and *or* in your sentences.

and, but, or	sing	play the guitar
I can sing **and** play the guitar.	✔	✔
I can't sing **or** play the guitar.	✗	✗
I can sing **but** I can't play the guitar.	✔	✗

*I can take photos and paint a picture. Luigi can't
speak Chinese or swim underwater.*

He can stand on his hands!

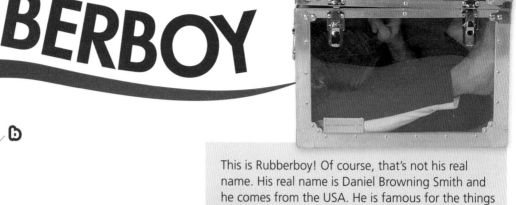

RUBBERBOY

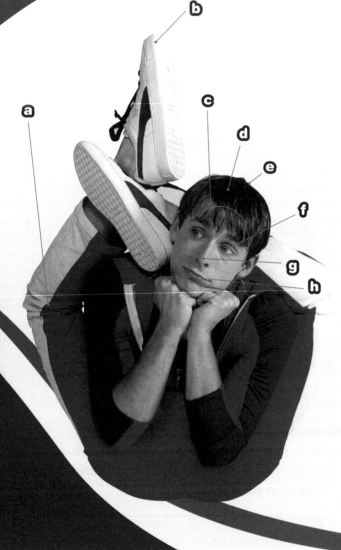

This is Rubberboy! Of course, that's not his real name. His real name is Daniel Browning Smith and he comes from the USA. He is famous for the things he can do with his body. For example, he can stand on his hands and put his feet behind his head. Can you do that? It's really difficult! He can also get into a very small box – just 34 cm × 40 cm × 50 cm. You can read about Daniel in a book called *Guinness World Records* and you can also see him in films and on TV.

VOCABULARY

1 Look at the photos. Match the parts of the body to the words in the box.

> arm   ear   eye   face   foot/feet   hair   hand
> head   leg   mouth   nose   tooth/teeth

▶1.41 Listen and check. Then repeat.

2 ▶1.42 Listen. Point to the parts of your body as you hear them.

3 Play the game in Exercise 2 with your partner.

READING

4 Read the article and answer the questions.

1 What is Rubberboy's real name?

2 Where is he from?

3 What is he famous for?

4 Where can you see Rubberboy?

GRAMMAR Prepositions *into, behind, under*

→ Grammar reference **page 141**

5 Match the sentences with the pictures.

Complete the sentences with *into, behind* or *under*.

0 His hands are ..... *behind* ..... his head. `b`

1 The guitar is .... the door. ☐

2 Put this book .... your bag. ☐

3 She is .... the table. ☐

4 His head is .... the desk. ☐

5 Get .... your bed! ☐

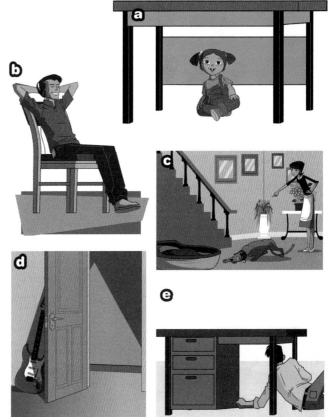

SPEAKING

6 Ask and answer with your partner.

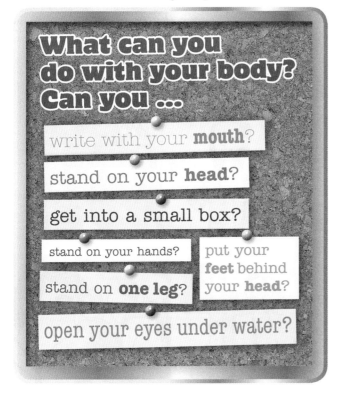

What can you do with your body? Can you ...

write with your **mouth**?

stand on your **head**?

get into a small box?

stand on your hands?

put your **feet** behind your **head**?

stand on **one leg**?

open your eyes under water?

7 Walk around the class. Ask and answer the questions in Exercise 6.

Hi, Sonia. Can you stand on your head?

Yes, I can. What about you?

No, I can't.

6 Party time!
Have we got any eggs?

bread
cheese ‒ for the cake
meat ‒ eggs
Milk ‒ flour
biscuits ‒ sugar
Fruit ‒ butter
apples ‒ Vegetables
bananas ‒ tomatoes
Oranges ‒ potatoes

VOCABULARY

1 Match the pictures to the things on the shopping list.

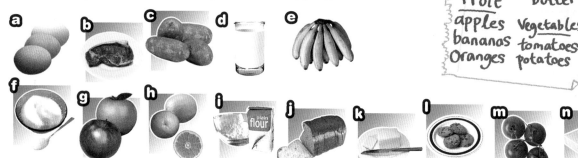

a b c d e
f g h i j k l m n

▶1.43 Listen and check. Then repeat.

1 Mum, can I make a birthday cake for Dad?

I don't know – have we got any eggs?

2 Er … no. Mum, we haven't got any food in the house.

OK. Let's go shopping.

3 Oh no! Look! There aren't any bananas!

Don't worry. There are lots of apples and oranges. Now, where are the things for the cake?

4 OK, Toby. We've got three eggs, some butter and some sugar and we've got lots of flour.

No, we don't need any cheese!

Oh no, Toby! Our cake! There's some on the floor and some on the walls and lots on your face! Have we got any left for Dad?

5 Hi Dad! Don't come in the kitchen!

6

7

8 Happy birthday, Dad!

▶1.44

2 Read the information in the box. Then write the things in Exercise 1 under the right basket.

There are things you can count (countable):
an apple   five apples
There are things you can't count (uncountable):
sugar
You can add *s* to countable nouns but you can't add *s* to uncountable nouns.

countable	uncountable
....apple....	....sugar....
....	....
....	....
....	....
....	....
....	....
....	

READING

3 Read the story and look at these sentences. Write *yes* or *no*.

0 Picture 1: It's Dad's birthday today.   *yes*
1 Picture 2: There's lots of food in the house.
2 Picture 3: Sally and Katie are at the supermarket.
3 Picture 4: Toby has got an egg in his hand.
4 Picture 5: Dad is in the kitchen.
5 Picture 6: Toby is on a chair.
6 Picture 7: Katie is happy.
7 Picture 8: Dad's birthday cake is very small.

GRAMMAR   *some, any, lots of*

Countable nouns	Uncountable nouns
➕	➕
We've got three eggs. There are some eggs. We've got lots of eggs.	We've got some flour. There's lots of flour.
➖	➖
We haven't got any eggs.	We haven't got any flour.
❓	❓
Have we got an egg? Have we got some/any eggs?	Have we got some/any flour?

→ Grammar reference **page 142**

4 Read the story again. Underline *some, any* and *lots of*.

5 Put the words in the right order to make questions and sentences.

0 got have chocolate you any ?
   Have you got any chocolate?
1 any we have biscuits got ?
2 got haven't milk we any .
3 there lots are of here eggs .
4 some banana got a I've oranges and .
5 lots we've of cheese got .
6 tomatoes haven't we any got .

PRONUNCIATION   *some*

6 ▶1.45 Listen to some sentences with *some*. Then listen again and repeat.

7 Look at the picture of the party food on page 124 and write sentences. Use *some*, *any* or *lots of*.

They've got some oranges.
They haven't got …
There's …

About you

8 Write a shopping list for *your* party.
9 Tell the people in your class about the food at your party.
   I've got lots of fruit. I haven't got any chocolate. I've got some cakes.

a

Can you come to
HANNAH'S PARTY?

Place: 33, Albert Street
Date: August 1st
Time: From 8 until late!
party food   games   dancing!
Call 020 875 645 or
email: Hannah.timms@worldnet.com

b

Please come to
Rebecca's party

on Wednesday, March 2nd
from 3.30 until 5.30
at Rebecca's house
Call 03276 753 902

c

Daniel invites you to come to his Swimming Party!

It's on Saturday, April 1st, at 2.15
Call Daniel – 01386 928704

d

Would you like to come to
MY PARTY?

It's on Saturday, July 1st, at Victoria
Park, from 10 am until 2 pm
Fun, food and football!
01792 894765   andrew@fgcool.com

READING

1 Read the invitations and find …

1 two different days.   Saturday ....
2 four different months.   ....
3 three different places.   ....
4 four different times.   ....
5 two email addresses.   ....
6 two phone numbers.   ....

LISTENING

2 ▶1.46 **Listen to the conversations and match them with an invitation (a–d).**

Conversation 1 ....   Conversation 3 ....
Conversation 2 ....   Conversation 4 ....

VOCABULARY

3 Look at the pictures. Match the times with the clocks.

0 It's six twenty.   f

1 It's 9 am.

2 It's one ten.

3 It's three thirty.

4 It's two fifteen.

5 It's four o'clock.

6 It's 7 pm.

▶1.47 Look at the clocks and listen. Then repeat.

4 ▶1.48 Listen and complete the clocks.

5 Ask and answer about the clocks in Exercise 3.

A: What time is it on clock a?

B: It's four o'clock.

GRAMMAR   Prepositions *on, at, from, until*

6 Read the invitations again. Underline *on*, *at*, *from* and *until*.

Then complete the table with *on*, *at*, *from* and *until*.

Days	......*on*...... Wednesday		
Times	.... 3.30 .... 5.30	.... 2.15	
Dates	.... August 1st		
Places	.... Rebecca's house		

→ Grammar reference **page 142**

7 Complete the sentences with *on*, *at*, *from* and *until*.

0 Tom's party's ......*on*...... Tuesday ......*at*...... 4.30.

1 Is your party .... July 1st?

2 The party is .... my house, ... 2 pm .... 5 pm.

3 See you .... the park .... Sunday!

4 My party is .... the swimming pool. It's .... 3 pm.

SPEAKING

8 Practise the conversations from Exercise 2 with your partner. You can find them on page 125. Change the days, times and places.

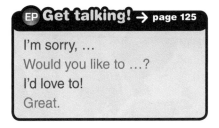

EP Get talking! → page 125

I'm sorry, …

Would you like to …?

I'd love to!

Great.

WRITING

9 Write an invitation to your party. Put

- the day
- the time
- the date
- the place
- your phone number and email address

Invite people to come to your party.

Would you like to …   What time …?

When …?   Where …?   It's on …   It's at …

I'd love to …   Oh, I'm sorry, I can't.

Culture
Holidays in the United States

fireworks

Christmas card

present

picnic

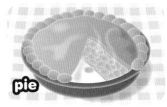
pie

pumpkin

turkey

parade

1 ▶1.49 Listen and repeat the words.

2 Which of the things from Exercise 1 can you see in the photographs?

PUBLIC HOLIDAYS IN THE USA

There are ten public holidays in the United States of America (USA). Here is some information about four of them.

Thanksgiving Fourth Thursday in November
This day is to say thank you for a good harvest.

> This is me and my family at Thanksgiving. Thanksgiving is a very important holiday in America. On the table you can see lots of food. There's a turkey, with potatoes and vegetables and for dessert we have pumpkin pie.

Independence Day July 4
This is a party for the birthday of the USA – the Declaration of Independence on July 4, 1776. It's also called 'The fourth of July'.

> The fourth of July is great fun. There are parades, parties and lots of fireworks. This is my grandmother in a parade in my town! You can see the US flag everywhere – in people's hands, on their clothes and on their homes.

Labor Day First Monday in September
This is a day for the USA's workers.

> This is my sister and me on Labor Day with our flags. On Labor Day there are parades, parties and family picnics. There are also football matches.

Christmas Day December 25

This is a very big holiday in the USA. It is a day for the birthday of Jesus Christ.

> At Christmas time, we send Christmas cards to our friends. There are lights on houses and in the streets. People have a tree in their living room, and there are presents for friends and family. There's also a big meal on Christmas day, with a turkey. Here's a photo of me and my sister. We're looking at the presents under the tree.

3 Read the information about holidays in the USA and look at the calendar. For this calendar, what *date* is:

Thanksgiving? Labor Day?

What *day* is:

Independence Day? Christmas Day?

4 Read about the holidays again. Then complete the table with ticks (✔) in the boxes.

	Thanksgiving	Independence Day	Labor Day	Christmas Day
presents				
big meal	✔			
parades				
fireworks				
cards				
parties				
football matches				
lights				
US flag				

5 Write some sentences about the holidays. Use the table to help you.

There are presents on Christmas Day.

6 Compare your sentences with your partner. Are they the same or different?

7 Answer these questions with a partner.

- Have you got a public holiday for workers in your country?
- Have you got a public holiday for independence?
- Have you got a public holiday to celebrate the harvest?
- When are they in your country?
- What are your favourite holidays in your country? Write their names and dates.

Project

Find some information about public holidays in another English-speaking country.
Look on the internet for information.
Write a list of the holidays.
Write the dates of the holidays.
Make a table like the one on this page.
Put four holidays into the table and then complete it.

7 Feeling good
I like playing basketball

VOCABULARY

1 Match the pictures to the words in the box.

> catching a ball   dancing   kicking a ball
> playing basketball   playing computer games
> playing football   playing tennis   running

▶1.50 Listen and check. Then repeat.

LISTENING

2 ▶1.51 Listen and write the names.

a ....'s photo
b ....'s photo
c ....'s photo

3 ▶1.51 Listen again and complete the sentences.
Then match the sentences to the pictures.

1 **Joelle:**   I'm not very good at ....
2 **Rosa:**   I'm good at ....

4 What are you good at? Tell your
partner.

A: *I'm good at swimming underwater but*
I'm not very good at catching a ball.
B: *I'm good at running and playing tennis.*

PRONUNCIATION Word stress

5 Underline the stress in the words.

0 <u>bas</u>ketball
1 computer
2 address
3 supermarket
4 potatoes
5 guitar
6 mother
7 bedroom
8 vegetables
9 tennis
10 nationality

▶1.52 **Listen and check. Then repeat.**

GRAMMAR like ⊕ ⊖

like / likes ☺		don't / doesn't like ☹	
I	like	I	don't like
you	like	you	don't like
she	likes	she	doesn't like
he	likes	he	doesn't like
we	like	we	don't like
you	like	you	don't like
they	like	they	don't like

→ Grammar reference **page 143**

6 Complete the sentences. ☺ = like / ☹ = not like

0 Ben ...._likes_............ ☺ kicking a ball in the park.
1 Mary .... ☹ dancing.
2 I .... ☺ playing computer games.
3 Alison and Gemma .... ☹ potatoes or bread.
4 You .... ☺ standing on your head.
5 Paul .... ☹ chocolate.
6 We .... ☺ learning English.

About you

7 Tick (✔) the table with information about you. Then add two more activities.

		I like	I don't like	I'm good at	I'm not very good at
0	playing tennis	✔			✔
1	playing computer games				
2	running				
3	playing basketball				
4	playing football				
5	dancing				
6	sport				
7	making cakes				
8	riding horses				
9	....				
10	....				

SPEAKING

8 Talk to two friends about the information in About you.

> I like playing tennis but I'm not very good at it. I don't like running.

> I like watching football but I don't like playing it. I'm good at dancing.

> I don't like running and I'm not very good at it. I like playing basketball.

WRITING

9 Now write about your friends.

Franka likes playing tennis but she doesn't like running. She isn't very good at computer games.

Giuseppe doesn't like running and he isn't very good at it. He likes playing basketball.

Eat a good breakfast!

ASK THE DOCTOR

1

Dear Doctor
I'm 15 years old and I'm not very happy. My friends like going to the park and playing football. I'm always tired. I can't go with them. I like watching sport on TV and I like playing computer games too. Is it good for me to stay at home? Can you help me?
Tim

a

Lots of sugar isn't good for us. It isn't good for our teeth! Eat more fruit and vegetables. You'll feel better.
Dr Smart

2

Dear Doctor
I'm 13 years old and I like eating chocolates and cakes. My mum isn't happy and gives me lots of fruit and vegetables but I don't like them. I do lots of things which are good for me. I like playing football and I'm very good at it. Is it OK for me to eat lots of sweet things?
Susie

b

It isn't good for you to stay at home all day. Go to the park and play football with your friends. You'll feel better.
Dr Smart

tip of the week

Eat a good breakfast.
* You'll do better in class.
* You'll do better at sport.
What is a good breakfast?
Choose the good breakfasts.
Answers are on page 125.

1 ☐

2 ☐

3 ☐

4 ☐

5 ☐

READING

1 Read the letters to the doctor. Match them to the doctor's answers.

2 Read the letters again and look at the sentences. Write *yes* or *no*.

0 Tim likes playing football. *no*
1 Susie likes eating apples.
2 Susie likes doing sport.
3 Tim likes going to the park.
4 Tim is very tired.
5 The doctor thinks it's good for Tim to stay at home.
6 The doctor thinks it's good for Susie to eat sweet things.

3 Read the doctor's 'tip of the week'. Look at the five breakfasts.

Tick (✔) three breakfasts which are good for you.

VOCABULARY

4 Work in pairs. Complete the table with words from the box. Add four of your ideas.

<del>biscuits</del> bread butter chocolate dancing
oranges playing computer games sugar
vegetables walking to school water

Good for you	Not good for you
	biscuits

About you

5 Write about your breakfast. Then tell your partner about it.

GRAMMAR   Pronouns

6 Read the letters and answers again. Can you find any of these words?

at it   for her   for him   for me   with them
for us   for you

→ Grammar reference page 143

7 Complete the table with the pronouns in red in Exercise 6.

I	....me....	we	....
you	....	you	....
he	....	they	....
she	....		
it	....		

8 Complete the sentences.

0 Eat a good breakfast. It's better for ....you..... .
1 They like playing basketball. It's good for ....
2 I like drinking milk. It's good for ....
3 She doesn't like eating ice cream. It isn't good for ....
4 We don't like eating a lot of chocolate. It isn't good for ....
5 He likes walking to school. It's good for ....

WRITING

9 Write a letter to the doctor. Use Tim and Susie's letters to help you.

10 Read your partner's letter and answer it. Use Dr Smart's answers to help you.

8 Things we do
She's dancing

AFTER-SCHOOL CLUBS:
OCTOBER – DECEMBER

THE CITY
SCHOOL

Monday	Tuesday	Wednesday	Thursday	Friday
street dancing ☐	guitar lessons ☐	photo club ☐	tennis lessons ☐	running club ☐
cooking ☐	film club ☐	drawing club ☐	horse riding ☐	football club ☐

a b c d e f g h i j

VOCABULARY

1 **Match the activities to the after-school clubs.**

a – running club

▶1.53 Listen and check. Then repeat.

2 **Look at the after-school clubs and choose (✔) one club for you for each day.**

Then work in groups of three. Talk about your after-school clubs. Take turns to speak.

> I've got photo club on Wednesday. What have you got?

> I've got photo club, too.

> I haven't got photo club. I've got drawing.

LISTENING

3 ▶1.54 Listen and write the day for each photo.

GRAMMAR Present continuous ➕ ➖

4 Look at examples a and b from the recording. Match them to 1 and 2.

> **a** Suzy says: I'm looking at some photos of me in my after-school clubs.
> **b** Suzy says: Look, I'm making a cake for my mum.
>
> **1** This is describing an action in a picture.
> **2** This is describing an action which is happening now.

→ Grammar reference **page 144**

→ Grammar reference **page 144**

5 Make sentences from the words in the circles. Compare your sentences with your partner.

Spelling

cook + ing = cooking ➝ He's cooking.
sit + t + ing = sitting ➝ He's sitting on his bed.
make + ing = making ➝ He's making films.

I'm you're
we're they're
he's she's it's

I'm not
you aren't we aren't
they aren't he isn't
she isn't it isn't

painting a picture
writing a letter
swimming kicking a ball
cooking a pizza
riding a horse

6 ▶1.55 Look at the picture and listen to the sentences.

Say *yes* or *no* for each sentence.

0 yes
1
2
3
4
5
6
7

Paul Ben Chris Carla Sally Freddy Susie Jane

READING AND WRITING

7 Read Martin's blog for the week. What's his favourite after-school activity?

8 Write a computer blog about you. Use Martin's blog to help you.

🗖🗙
Day: Friday 14 October. Time: 18:43

I'm at home and I'm sitting on my bed. I've got new activities after school every day. I like making films. It's really cool. I don't like the swimming club. I want to change to cooking. Then I can eat lots! I'm always hungry.
Text me. I'm bored!
Martin

Are you making lunch?

READING AND VOCABULARY

1 **What are they doing? Read the story and complete the sentences.**

1 Nat is ....
2 Katie is ....
3 Jason is ....

1.56

2 Read the story again and complete the diagram with words from the box.

.... your homework

make   do

....

> the cleaning   lunch   your bed
> ~~your homework~~

About you

3 What do you do in your house? Make a list and compare with your partner.
clean my bedroom
wash the car

GRAMMAR   Present continuous ❓

4 Read the story again. First complete the table with Sally's questions (Q). Then write the answers (A) to Sally's questions in the table.

> Q: Are you .... your bed?
> A: ....
> Q: Are you doing your .... ?
> A: ....
> Q: Are you .... the cleaning?
> A: ....

→ Grammar reference **page 144**

▶ 1.57 Listen and check.

5 Complete the sentences with the verbs (in brackets).

0   ..Are.. you ....making..... (make) your bed?
    No, ...I'm not..... .

1   .... Lucy .... (clean) her bedroom?
    Yes, ...

2   .... you .... (make) a cake?
    No, ...

3   .... they .... (eat) lunch?
    No, ...

4   .... Peter .... (wash) the car?
    Yes, ...

PRONUNCIATION   *Yes / No* questions

6 ▶ 1.58 Listen and repeat the questions.

A: *Are you washing the car?*
B: *No, we aren't.*

B: *Is Nat helping in the kitchen?*
A: *Yes, he is.*

7 Look at the story again for one minute. Then close your book. Ask and answer with your partner.

A: *Is Nat doing his homework?*
B: *Yes, he is.*
A: *No, he isn't. He's making his bed.*

B: *Is Jason making lunch?*
A: *Yes, he is.*
B: *Right!*

8 Work in groups of four. Act the story.

SPEAKING

9 Work in groups of three.

Student A mimes an activity. Students B and C ask questions to guess the activity.

B: *Are you running?*
A: *No, I'm not.*
C: *Are you riding a horse?*
A: *Yes, I am!*

Science
Robots

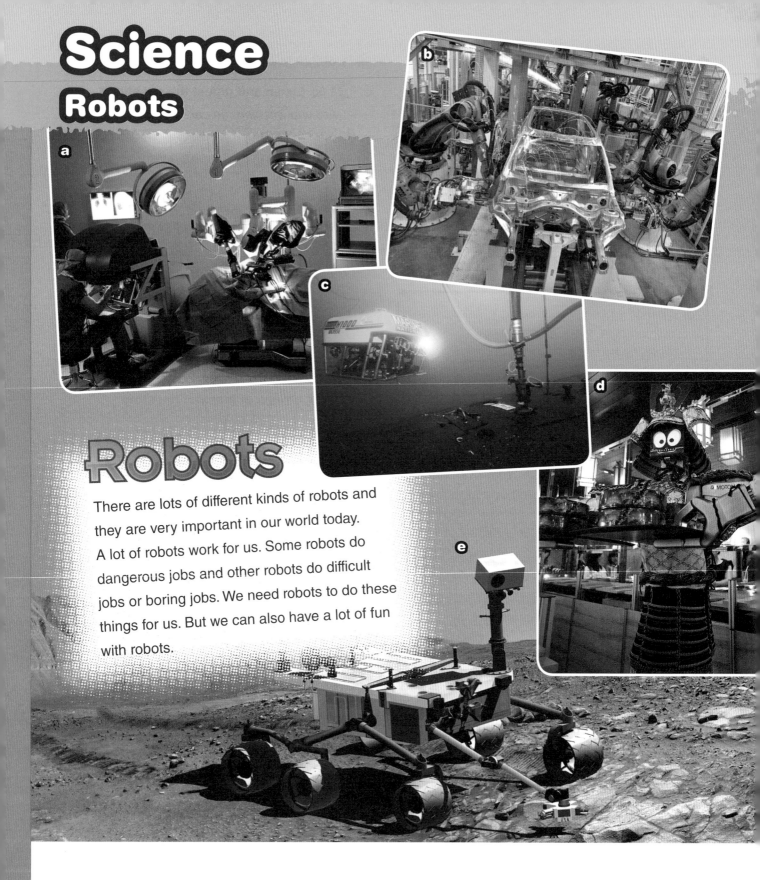

Robots

There are lots of different kinds of robots and they are very important in our world today. A lot of robots work for us. Some robots do dangerous jobs and other robots do difficult jobs or boring jobs. We need robots to do these things for us. But we can also have a lot of fun with robots.

1 Read the text. Why do we have robots?

2 Match the robots with these jobs.

0	make cars	robot b
1	work in a café	....
2	move under water	....
3	work in a hospital	....
4	explore different planets	....

3 Which of the robot's jobs in Exercise 2 are *dangerous*, *difficult*, *boring* or *fun*?

4 Look at the photos of the robots and find these things.

1 a camera
2 wheels
3 arms
4 a hand

5 ▶1.59 **Listen to some information about four robots. Match the robots to the photos.**

Repliee Q1   Asimo   Carp Robot   Spykee

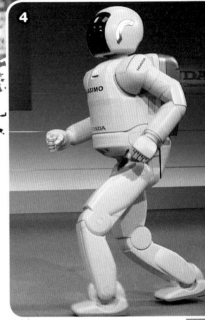

6 ▶1.59 **Listen again. One sentence for each robot is wrong. Find the wrong sentence and correct it.**

Repliee Q1 has got a beautiful face.
She can move her face and arms.
She can walk.

Carp robot is blue and silver.
It hasn't got a camera in its head.
It can give information about the water.

Asimo can't run.
Asimo can understand people's faces.
Asimo can open doors.

Spykee can take photos and make phone calls.
Spykee can't move.
Spykee can see and hear.

Project

Design and draw a robot. Think about these questions.
  1 What can it do? (swim? walk? run? … ?)
  2 What has it got? (arms? legs? wheels? a camera? … ?)
  3 What is it for? (doing your homework? exploring planets? … ?)
Work in a group. Tell each other about your robots.

My robot is called …
It's got …
It can …   and …
It can't …   or …

Review 2
Units 5–8

VOCABULARY

1 Circle the odd word out.

0 September March (Monday) July
1 apple banana potato orange
2 running catching kicking standing
3 biscuits chocolate cake vegetables
4 washing dancing cleaning cooking
5 fruit milk cheese butter
6 foot mouth teeth hair

2 Label the pictures with the parts of the body.

1 ....
2 ....
3 ....
4 ....
5 ....
6 ....
7 ....
8 ....
9 ....
10 ....
11 ....
12 ....

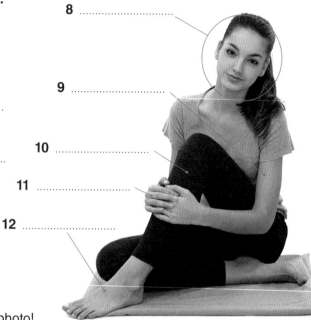

GRAMMAR

3 Complete the sentences.

0 Say cheese! They 're taking (take) our photo!
1 Sorry, I can't talk now. I .... (have) a shower.
2 Hey! You .... (sit) on my bag.
3 She .... (not do) her homework. She .... (watch) TV.
4 .... he .... (help) his dad? No, he ....
5 What .... they .... (eat)?
6 We .... (not play). We .... (make) a film.
7 Listen! My brother .... (practise) the piano.
8 .... you .... (wear) your new T-shirt?
9 They .... (not ride) their bikes. They .... (walk).

4 Look at the shopping and correct the sentences.
Use *some*, *any* or *lots of*.

0 They've got lots of potatoes.
  They haven't got any potatoes.
1 They've got some chocolate biscuits.
2 They haven't got any fruit.
3 They haven't got any drinks.
4 They've got lots of bread.
5 They haven't got any meat.
6 They've got some tomatoes.
7 They've got lots of cheese.

5 Look at the table and make sentences. Use *can / can't* and *and/but/or*.

	play tennis	swim	run fast	cook	paint	speak Russian	speak French	play the guitar
Jim					✔			✗
Maria		✗	✔					
Sara		✗	✗					
Rose						✔	✔	
Callum	✔			✗				
Anita	✗							✗

Jim can paint but he can't play the guitar.

LISTENING

6 ▶1.60 Listen to Simon's phone calls. Where's Simon? What's he doing? Listen again and complete the table.

		Can he/she talk to Simon?	What is he/she doing?	Is Simon happy?
1	Jane			
2	Ben			
3	Mina			
4	Alex			

READING

7 Read about Jimmy. Then read sentences 1–8 and write *yes* or *no*.

Jimmy's twelve. He's got one brother and one sister. Jimmy's brother is fifteen and his name's Sam. His sister is ten and her name is Jess. Jimmy's sister likes reading and doesn't like playing sports. His brother doesn't like reading and he doesn't like playing sport. He likes cooking and playing the guitar. Jimmy isn't very good at cooking but he likes playing tennis.

0 Jimmy is fifteen.   no

1 There are three children in Jimmy's family.

2 Sam is fifteen.

3 Jimmy's sister is called Jess.

4 Jess and Sam are brothers.

5 Jess likes playing sports.

6 Sam doesn't like reading.

7 Sam likes cooking.

8 Jimmy doesn't like playing sport.

SPEAKING

8 Complete the invitation on page 129.

Walk around the class and invite people to your party.

Ask them to bring some food.

Complete the table.

Who can come?	What can they bring?

9 My day
I get up at 7 o'clock

LISTENING

1 ▶ 1.61 **Listen and answer the questions.**

1 Is Rosa happy?
2 Is José good at taking photos?
3 What day is the photo club?
4 What has José got at five o'clock?

2 ▶ 1.61 **Complete the sentences with the words in the box. Then listen again and check.**

can   can't   ~~clothes~~   different
every day   teeth

0 José's ....clothes........ are new.
1 The next photo club project is 'Things we do ....'
2 You clean your .... in the morning.
3 José .... go to the next photo club with his friends.
4 José .... go for a drink.
5 José's day is .... from Rosa's day.

VOCABULARY

3 **Look at the things you do in the morning. Match the pictures to the words in the box.**

clean your teeth   leave the house
get dressed   walk to school
catch the bus to school   get up
have breakfast   wake up   wash your face

▶ 1.62 **Listen and check. Then repeat.**

4 ▶1.63 **Listen to Rosa and José and read. Two things are different from the recording. What are they?**

Rosa On Mondays I wake up, get up and wash my face. Then I get dressed and have breakfast with my dad. Then I clean my teeth, put my things in my school bag and catch the bus to school. I go to school at eight thirty.

José On Mondays I wake up, get up and wash my face. I have breakfast in my room and then I clean my teeth. At two o'clock I put my things in my bag and leave the hotel. I go to school at five o'clock.

GRAMMAR   Present simple ⊕

I get up **and** get dressed. Rosa gets up **and** gets dressed. She catches **the** bus to school.

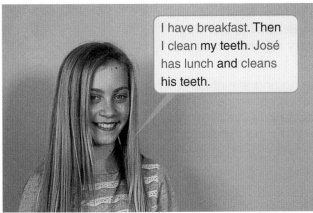

I have breakfast. **Then** I clean **my** teeth. José has lunch **and** cleans his teeth.

We go to school at eight thirty. José goes to school at five o'clock.

→ Grammar reference **page 145**

5 **Make correct sentences from the box.**

I go to school at eight o'clock.

I you he she we you they	catches the bus to school clean our teeth gets up at seven o'clock go to school at eight o'clock has breakfast at seven thirty get dressed walk to school wash my face

PRONUNCIATION   Present simple endings

6 ▶1.64 **Listen and complete the table.**

cleans   makes   paints   washes
plays   swims   walks   watches

/s/ **gets**	/z/ **runs**	/ɪz/ **catch**es

▶1.65 **Listen and check. Then repeat.**

SPEAKING

About you

7 Tell your partner what you do in the mornings.
I get up and have breakfast with my mum and dad. Then I clean my teeth and get dressed.

8 Tell the class about your partner.
A: *Carolina gets up and washes her face.*
B: *Miguel has breakfast and then cleans his teeth.*

WRITING

9 **Write about what your partner does in the mornings before school.**

Laura gets up at eight o'clock and has breakfast. Then she washes her face, cleans her teeth and gets dressed.

I don't sleep at night

VOCABULARY

1 **What's the time?**

 0
 1
 2
 3

It's half past nine.

 4
 5
 6
 7

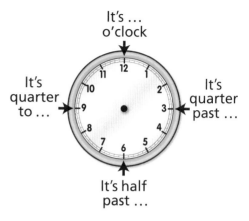

It's … o'clock

It's quarter to … →

It's quarter past … ←

It's half past …

2 ▶1.66 **Draw six clocks in your notebook. Listen and draw the time on each one.**

READING

3 **Read Christine's blog and answer the questions.**

What does Christine do at …

1 4.15 in the afternoon?   **3** 9.30 in the evening?   **5** 5.45 am?
2 5.30 pm?   **4** 5.15 am?

My Brazil blog

Hi. My name's Christine and I'm from Scotland. But I'm not in Scotland now. I'm in Brazil. I'm working with animals. My life here is very different from my life in Scotland!

Here in Brazil, I work in the evening and at night and I sleep in the day! I get up at about 4 pm and at 4.15 I have breakfast with the other students. After breakfast, at about 5.30 in the afternoon, we put our things into our bags. At 6 pm we go into the forest and look for birds.

We write their names in our notebooks. We don't talk because we don't want the birds to hear us. At 9.30 in the evening we stop and eat sandwiches and drink water or juice. It's our lunch! We don't stop for a long time. At about 10.15 we look for night animals.

We finish at about 3 am. Before we eat our dinner, we write the names of all the birds and animals on the computer. We have dinner at 5.15. At 5.45 in the morning, I'm very tired. I'm ready for bed!

I don't see the sun because I sleep all day! But this is a great job and I'm very happy.

4 **Read the blog again and complete the sentences. Use the words in the box.**

> at night ~~Brazil~~ goes in the evening looks for
> names ~~Scotland~~ sleeps tired to bed

0 Christine is from ...Scotland... but now she is in .....Brazil......

1 She works .... and .... and she .... in the day.

2 She .... into the forest and .... birds and night animals.

3 She writes the .... of the birds and the night animals in her notebook.

4 After dinner she goes .... She is very ....

GRAMMAR Present simple ⊖

> In Brazil, Christine sleeps in the day. She doesn't sleep at night. The students don't see the sun.

> Here in Brazil I work in the evening. I don't work in the evening in Scotland.

> We don't stop for a long time to eat our lunch.

→ Grammar reference **page 145**

5 ▶ 1.67 **Listen and repeat.**

6 **Talk about things Christine doesn't do in Scotland.**

0 have breakfast
In Brazil, Christine has breakfast at quarter past four. She doesn't have breakfast at quarter past four in Scotland.

1 get up
2 have lunch
3 have dinner
4 go to bed

7 **Complete the sentences with the verbs (in brackets).**

0 You ......don't live...... (not live) in Scotland.

1 My sister .... (not wash) her hair in the morning.

2 My mum and dad .... (not make) sandwiches for lunch.

3 I .... (not do) my homework in the morning before school.

4 James .... (not get) the bus to school.

5 We .... (not go) to school on Sundays.

6 My teacher .... (not work) at night.

SPEAKING

About you

8 Read about Themba. How is your day different? Tell your partner what you do and don't do.
I don't get up at quarter past six in the morning. I get up at seven o'clock.

> **Hi. My name's Themba.** I'm sixteen and I'm from South Africa.

Morning
☺ 6.15 get up
☺ 7.00 walk to the Football Academy
☺ 7.30 play and learn about football
☺ 9.30 have breakfast
☺ 10.00 play a football game

Afternoon
☺ 12.00 have lunch
☺ 12.30 go to school for lessons
☺ 4.00 have a drink and a sandwich
☺ 4.30 play football with friends in the park
☺ 6.30 eat with my family

Evening
☺ 7.00 do homework
☺ 10.00 go to bed

WRITING

9 **Write sentences about how your partner's day is different from Themba's day.**

Manuela doesn't go to a Football Academy. She goes to a high school.
She gets up at seven o'clock. She doesn't get up at quarter past six.

10 Information
Do we have art on Fridays?

VOCABULARY

1 Look at the pictures. Put the letters in the right order to make the school subjects.

▶ **1.68** Listen and check. Then repeat.

1 suMic
Music

2 ceinceS

3 naSpish

4 praGeoghy

5 ishglEn

6 TI

7 rAt

8 toryisH

2+6=8
3×7=21
6+2-3=5
360 ÷ 12 = 30

9 EP

10 sthaM

About you

2 Complete the sentences.
- My favourite subjects are …
- I'm good at …
- I'm not very good at …
- I really like …
- I don't like …

Talk to your partner about the subjects.

A: I really like music and I'm good at PE.

B: I'm good at PE too but I don't like music. My favourite subject is IT.

A: I'm not very good at art. My favourite subject is PE.

READING

1

Hey, Nat. Look. Do you understand this science question?

Let me look … aargh … No, I don't. Sorry. I don't like science. It's difficult!

2

I've got a test tomorrow. Does Dad like science?

Yes, he does. He loves it! He can help you!

Good idea! Dad …

3

No, I don't.

Thanks, Dad! … Hey, Nat! My homework is finished. Do you want to play a game on the computer?

4

Katie, do you like art?

Does Toby like art?

Well, you can do some painting with Toby, then.

Yes, I do. I love it. It's my favourite subject. It's easy.

Yes, he does.

Oh, Dad!

▶ 1.69

3 **Read the story and answer the questions.**

1 Who likes science?
2 Who doesn't like science?
3 Who likes art?

4 **Read the story again and number the sentences in order.**

☐ Katie doesn't want to paint with her baby brother.
☐ Katie asks her dad to help her.
☐ Katie doesn't understand her homework.
☐ Katie wants to play on the computer.

GRAMMAR Present simple ❓

5 **Underline questions in the story which start with *Do* or *Does*.**

Then underline the short answers.

▶1.70 **Listen and check.**

6 **Choose the right word to complete the sentences about the present simple.**

1 We use do / does to make questions and short answers with *he* and *she*.
2 We use do / does to make questions and short answers with *I, you, we* and *they*.

→ Grammar reference **page 146**

7 **Look at Katie's school timetable and complete questions and answers 1–3. Then answer questions 4–5 with information about you.**

0 **A:** ..Does..Katie..have.. geography on Tuesdays?
  B: Yes, ...she does............. .
1 **A:** .... science on Wednesdays?
  B: ....
2 **A:** .... art on Fridays?
  B: ....
3 **A:** .... history on Mondays?
  B: ....
4 **A:** Do you have English on Thursdays?
  B: ....
5 **A:** Do you have maths on Wednesdays?
  B: ....

▶1.71 **Listen and check.**

SPEAKING

8 **Make questions. Then ask and answer with your partner.**

0 you / go to school / on Saturdays?
A: Do you go to school on Saturdays?
B: Yes, I do.
1 you / do homework / in the morning?
2 you / understand / your maths lessons?
3 you / use IT / in English lessons?
4 your dad / help you / with homework?
5 your school / have / a photo club?
6 your teacher / walk / to school?
7 your friend / like PE?
8 your mum and dad / speak English?

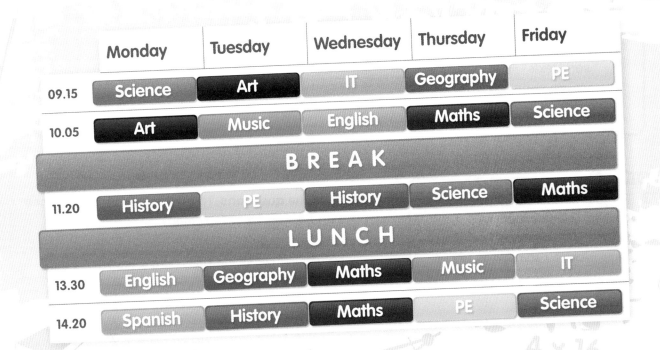

	Monday	Tuesday	Wednesday	Thursday	Friday
09.15	Science	Art	IT	Geography	PE
10.05	Art	Music	English	Maths	Science
	B R E A K				
11.20	History	PE	History	Science	Maths
	L U N C H				
13.30	English	Geography	Maths	Music	IT
14.20	Spanish	History	Maths	PE	Science

How many texts do you send?

a computer

b smartphone

c memory stick

d digital camera

e tablet

VOCABULARY

1 Match the activities to the things in the photos. Some things have more than one activity.

1 download music
2 look at websites
3 read and send emails
4 watch films
5 read and send texts
6 take photos
7 store information

LISTENING

2 ▶1.72 Listen to four people talking about the things in the photos. Write the things under the right person.

What do they do with them? Listen again and complete the table.

	Tania	Bruno	Daniela	Victor
	tablet			
download music				
look at websites				
send emails				
watch films	✔			
send texts				
take photos				
store information				

About you

3 Tell your partner about your things. What do you use them for?
I've got a smartphone. I send texts to my friends. I sometimes phone my family.

GRAMMAR *How much ...? / How many ...?*

4 Read the questions. Then complete the sentences with *how much* or *how many*.

How many texts do you get in a day?
How much TV do you watch in a week?

We use .... with countable nouns.
We use .... with uncountable nouns.

→ Grammar reference **page 146**

5 Choose the right words to complete the questions. Then tick (✔) the answers for you.

1 *How many / How much fruit do you eat in a week?*
   1 I eat lots.
   2 I eat some.
   3 I don't eat any.

2 *How many / How much books have you got in your bag?*
   1 I've got lots.
   2 I haven't got any.
   3 I've got four.

3 *How many / How much bread do you eat in a day?*
   1 I don't eat any.
   2 I eat some.
   3 I eat lots.

4 *How many / How much tennis do you play in a week?*
   1 I play some.
   2 I play lots.
   3 I don't play any.

5 *How many / How much computer games have you got?*
   1 I've got ten.
   2 I haven't got any.
   3 I've got some.

6 *How many / How much cooking do you do at home?*
   1 I do lots.
   2 I do some.
   3 I don't do any.

6 Ask and answer the quiz questions with your partner.

A: *How much fruit do you eat in a week?*
B: *I eat lots.*

SPEAKING

7 Make a table like the one below. Make six questions from the words in the boxes and write them in the table.

emails   websites   photos
computer games   texts

television   music   homework

do   write   listen to
send   visit   watch   take
get   play   have

in a day?   at the weekend?
in a week?   in a month?
on your phone?

	Questions	Me	Juan	George	Tatiana
	How many emails do you send in a week?	*0*	*lots*	*4*	*some*
1					
2					
3					

8 Complete the *Me* column of the table with information about you.

Then ask three friends. Put their names at the top of the table and write short answers.

A: *Juan, how many emails do you send in a week?*
B: *I'm not sure. I send lots of emails.*

A: *OK. How many emails do you send, George?*
C: *I send about four emails in a week.*

A: *Right. How many emails do you send, Tatiana?*
D: *I don't know. I send some.*

9 Tell your class about your friends.

Juan sends lots of emails in a week, but he doesn't visit any websites.
George sends about four emails in a week and plays some computer games at the weekend.
Tatiana listens to lots of music on her phone. She also takes lots of photos.

WRITING

10 Write four things about your friends. Use *and, but* and *also.*

Culture
The School of the Air

PART 1

In some parts of the world, students cannot go to school because there isn't a school near their home.

In Australia, some of these students go to the 'School of the Air'. The School of the Air isn't a real school. It's an internet school. The students have lessons, watch DVDs and videos, talk to their teacher and to other students. They do all this on computers. This is also called 'e-learning' or electronic learning.

PART 2

Frank is twelve years old. He hasn't got any brothers or sisters. He lives with his mother and father on a farm in the centre of Australia. There isn't a town or a school near his house, so Frank goes to the School of the Air.

He gets up at six in the morning and helps his dad on the farm and then, after breakfast, he sits at his computer and waits for his first lesson to start. He can see his teacher on screen and his teacher uses an interactive whiteboard. This helps Frank to understand the lesson. Then he can save the documents from the interactive whiteboard to his computer and read them again after the lesson. Frank's got a microphone and headphones so he can hear and talk to the teacher and to the other students in the class. His teacher's got a webcam.

At the end of the lesson, the teacher gives Frank some homework and a project to do before the next lesson.

Frank studies for about five hours a day and his mum and dad help him with his homework and his lessons. He uses videos from the internet and different websites to help him learn. His teachers also send him books to read.

In the summer, Frank meets some of the other students. They go to camp and have fun together for a week.

1 Read Part 1. Choose the correct words to complete the sentences.

0 The School of the Air is in *Australia* / *Canada*.

1 The students in the School of the Air study *in a classroom* / *on computers*.

2 E-learning is *learning on the internet* / *learning in a classroom*.

2 Read Part 2. Then read the sentences and write *yes* or *no*.

0 Frank starts his lessons at six o'clock.   *no*

1 There are two people in Frank's family.

2 Frank can see his teacher on his computer.

3 Frank talks to other students on the phone.

4 Frank has projects to do after the lessons.

5 Frank does his homework with his mum and dad.

6 Frank has a holiday in the winter with some of the students.

3 Match the technology words in the box to the definitions.

headphones   interactive whiteboard
microphone   screen   video   webcam

1 We put these on or in our ears to hear music or people speaking.

2 We talk into this. Then people can hear us.

3 This is the part of a computer where we can see the text and pictures.

4 This is an internet camera.

5 This is a kind of film.

6 A teacher uses this in the classroom. It's a board and a computer.

Project

Choose one of these ideas for your project.

1 You've got a webcam at home.
  - Put some of your favourite things near the computer at home in front of the webcam.
  - Make a video of your things. Record your voice describing your things as you film them.
  - Email the video to your teacher.
  - Look at the video on the school computer with your friends.
  - Tell your friends about the things in the video.

2 You've got a webcam at school.
  - Work in pairs.
  - Write ten simple questions to ask each other.
  - Turn on the webcam.
  - Record your interviews.
  - Watch the interviews together on the computer and show them to the class.

11 He's famous
I always read my emails

LISTENING

1 **Look at the photo and answer the questions.**

1 Who can you see in the photo?

2 What's happening?

2 ▶2.02 **Read the sentences about José. Then listen to José answering questions on TV. Write *yes* or *no*.**

1 José is watching TV.

2 José is famous in Brazil.

3 José is living in Britain now.

4 José plays tennis every day.

5 José often uses the internet.

6 José likes listening to music.

7 José watches a lot of TV.

8 José answers all the emails from his fans.

VOCABULARY

3 **Match the words and the meanings. You can use a dictionary to help you.**

1 fans	g	**a**	you can watch this every week
2 band		**b**	some people read this every morning
3 TV show		**c**	lots of people know about him or her
4 newspaper		**d**	these people make music together
5 famous person		**e**	another word for film
6 song		**f**	you go to this to see people making music
7 movie		**g**	these people like a person or a sport a lot
8 concert		**h**	music and words

▶2.03 **Listen and repeat.**

4 ▶2.02 **Listen to the conversation in Exercise 2 again. Tick (✔) the words in Exercise 3 when you hear them. You don't hear one word.**

5 **Ask and answer with your partner.**

GRAMMAR Adverbs of frequency: *always, often, sometimes, never*

6 **Read the examples from the recording and write the words in red under the right picture.**

I like watching tennis but I don't play it. I never do any sports.
I love taking photographs. I always have my camera with me.
I like using the computer. I often go on the internet.
I don't watch much TV but I sometimes watch the chart show.

a .... b .... c .... d ....

→ Grammar reference **page 147**

7 **Choose the correct word in blue.**

We put *always*, *often*, *sometimes* and *never* before / after most verbs.

8 **Write the sentences with an adverb of frequency in the right place. Use the pictures to help you.**

0 My brother sleeps until half past eleven.
   My brother always sleeps until half past eleven.

1 My dad helps me with my science homework.

2 I play computer games after school.

3 My friend sends me very long text messages.

4 I take my phone to school.

5 I ride my horse at the weekend.

▶2.04 **Listen and check. Then repeat.**

About you

9 Complete the sentences with *always*, *often*, *sometimes* or *never*. Compare your answers with your partner.
   1 I .... help my mum in the kitchen.
   2 I .... listen to music in the morning.
   3 I .... get up before 7 o'clock.
   4 I .... wash the car at the weekend.
   5 I .... remember my friends' birthdays.
   6 I .... do my homework in bed.
   7 I .... clean the bathroom.
   8 I .... forget to clean my teeth at night.

Sebastian Perez is a very exciting young tennis player. Here, we ask him some questions about his life.

Do your parents play tennis too?
No, my parents can't play tennis, but they help me a lot. They drive me to the tennis club and they always watch me play.

Sebastian, where do you come from?
I come from Argentina but I play tennis in other countries too, for example Brazil and Colombia.

Who is your favourite tennis player?
My favourite is the Spanish player, Rafael Nadal. I'm a big fan of his. I like Juan Martin Del Potro too – he comes from Argentina like me.

How often do you practise?
I practise every day. Sometimes I miss lessons but the teacher always gives me the work and I try to do it.

When do you go out with your friends?
Well, I see my friends at school but I don't often go out with them. I haven't got time! But they sometimes come to my house after school and we play computer games together.

What things do you like eating?
I love chocolate but I don't eat sweet things very often because they're not good for me. I eat lots of fruit and vegetables and I drink lots of water.

Do you want to be famous one day?
Of course I do! I want to be a really great tennis player when I'm an adult.

READING

1 Read about Sebastian Perez and choose the right words to complete the sentences.

0 Sebastian comes from *Brazil* / *Argentina*.

1 Sebastian's parents *can* / *can't* play tennis.

2 Sebastian's favourite tennis player is *Rafael Nadal* / *Juan Martin Del Potro*.

3 Sebastian *practises* / *doesn't practise* every day.

4 Sebastian *sometimes* / *never* plays computer games with his friends.

5 Sebastian *eats* / *doesn't eat* lots of chocolate.

GRAMMAR *Wh-* questions

2 **Match the question words with the answers.**

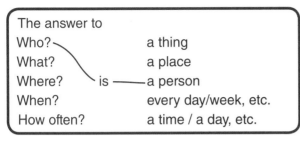

The answer to
Who? ———— a thing
What? ———— a place
Where? — is — a person
When? ———— every day/week, etc.
How often? ———— a time / a day, etc.

→ **Grammar reference page 147**

3 **Complete the questions.**

1 .... do you live?
2 ....'s your best friend?
3 .... does your favourite TV show start?
4 .... do you clean your bedroom?
5 ....'s your favourite sport?

PRONUNCIATION *Wh-* questions

4 ▶2.05 **Listen to the *Wh-* questions from Exercise 3. Does the voice go up (↗) or down (↘)?**

5 ▶2.06 **Listen again and repeat. Then ask and answer the questions with your partner.**

VOCABULARY

Some words in English have more than one meaning, for example *catch*.
I ***catch*** the bus at 7.30 every morning.
Can you ***catch*** a ball?
How do you say these sentences in your language? Do you use *catch* for both sentences?

6 **Complete each pair of sentences with a word from the box.**

comes get meet see things think

0 a Sebastian ......*comes*...... from Argentina.
 b My friend sometimes ......*comes*...... to my house.
1 a What do you .... of Justin Bieber's new song?
 b I .... the party starts at 6 o'clock.
2 a I .... my friends at school every day.
 b Excuse me. I can't .... the board.
3 a Don't forget your swimming ....!
 b My brother loves eating sweet ....
4 a I often .... my friends in town.
 b Hello, Sam. Nice to .... you.
5 a What time do you .... home?
 b We need to .... some bread.

SPEAKING

7 **Work with a partner. Write 10 questions to ask a famous person.**

What / favourite band / movie / TV show?
What kind of sports / food …?
Where / meet friends?
How often / go out / see friends?
What time / get up / go to bed?
When / read emails / watch TV?
What / think of …?

8 **Work with a partner. Take turns to be a famous person. Ask and answer the questions in Exercise 7 with your partner.**

12 Working life
What does she do?

This is my dad. He's a doctor. He works in a big hospital. But he's not at work today. Today he's in the sea with my sister. She's learning how to swim underwater.

This is my dad's friend Tony. Tony's got an interesting job. He's a driver. He drives all over Europe. He sometimes goes to Africa too! Today he's trying to catch a fish!

This is my mum. She's a music teacher. She teaches children to play the guitar. She isn't teaching now. She's eating a big ice cream.

This is Amanda. She's Tony's wife. She's a waitress. She works in a restaurant every evening. She isn't working now. She's taking a photo of Tony.

Hi, Sue here. We're having a great holiday! Let's see what everyone's doing today.

This is my brother Jim. He's a student. He's got an important test next week. But he isn't studying now. He's sleeping in the sun. Jim sleeps a lot but he never studies!

READING

1 **Read about Sue's family again and answer the questions.**

0 Who is Jim?   He's Sue's brother.

1 Does Jim like sleeping?

2 Can Sue's mum play the guitar?

3 Where is Sue's dad now?

4 What is Tony doing?

5 When does Amanda work?

VOCABULARY

2 **Find these words in the text. Are they verbs or nouns? Put them in the correct column. One word goes in both columns.**

doctor drive driver job learn student study teacher test waitress work

Nouns	Verbs
doctor	

▶2.07 **Listen and check. Then repeat.**

3 **Make ten true sentences. Compare with your partner.**

A student takes tests.

A student
A teacher
A driver
A waitress
A doctor

takes tests.
gives people their food.
makes people feel better.
learns interesting things.
sits a lot.
walks a lot.
gives children tests.
helps people to learn.
cleans tables.
reads and writes all day.

4 ▶2.08 **Listen and say *yes* or *no*.**

0 no   **1**   **2**   **3**   **4**   **5**

GRAMMAR Present simple and present continuous

5 **Look at sentences A and B.**

A He works in a big hospital. (present simple)
B He's swimming today. (present continuous)

Now look at all the verbs in red on page 72. Which are like A and which are like B?

6 **Complete the sentences with *present simple* or *present continuous*.**

We use the
.... to talk about what
we do every day.
We use the .... to talk
about what we always/sometimes/never do.
We use the .... to talk
about what we are doing now.

→ Grammar reference **page 148**

7 **Complete the conversations with the verbs (in brackets). Use the present simple or present continuous.**

Sue: Has your brother got a job?
Dan: Yes, he has. He (1) ....
(drive) a taxi.
Sue: Really? (2) .... he ....
(drive) you to school every day?
Dan: No, of course not!

Tim: What does your dad do?
Lee: He (3) .... (work) in a
restaurant.
Tim: That's interesting.
Lee: But he (4) .... (not work)
now. He (5) .... (cook) our
dinner.
Tim: Oh, good!

Jess: Hi, Millie. It's Jess here. I'm in Jamaica.
What (6) .... you ....
(do)?
Millie: I'm in bed!
Jess: Oh, sorry! I (7) .... (sit) by
the sea and I (8) .... (eat)
a big ice cream.
Millie: Lovely!

▶2.09 **Listen and check.**

8 **Practise the conversations in Exercise 7 with your partner.**

Can you work in my café?

READING

1 Read the story. Choose the correct word.

Picture 1: Jason thinks it's *easy / difficult* to be a waiter.

Picture 3: Jason thinks it's *easy / difficult* to be a waiter.

2 Read the story again and match the questions to the answers.

1 Who wants a drink?	a	Table 1
2 Who wants some food?	b	Table 2
3 Who has a dirty table?	c	Table 3

▶2.10

GRAMMAR *can:* requests and permission

3 **Match sentences 1–3 with a–c.**

1 Can I have some coffee, please?	a He wants to do something.
2 Can I go home now, please?	b She is asking for something.
3 Can you clean this table, please?	c He is asking a person to do something.

→ Grammar reference **page 148**

4 **Complete A's questions with *Can I* or *Can you*. Then write B's answers:**
Sure, no problem. / OK. / Yes, of course.

0 A: ...*Can you*... buy me a new football, please?   B: ...*Ok*...................................

1 A: .... watch TV, please, Dad?   B: ....

2 A: .... use your camera? I want to take a   B: ....
photo of that bird.

3 A: .... put these books on the table, please?   B: ....

4 A: .... help me with my homework?   B: ....

5 A: .... have an egg for breakfast, Mum?   B: ....

6 A: .... meet me in the park after school?   B: ....

VOCABULARY

5 **Match the pictures with things on the menu in picture 1.**

0

1

fish

2

3

4

5

6

7

8

▶2.11 **Listen and check. Then repeat.**

About you

6 Write five sentences about you. Compare with your partner.
For lunch, I sometimes/often have …
My favourite food is …
I sometimes/often/never go to cafés …
I like / don't like …
When I go to a café, I have …

LISTENING AND SPEAKING

7 ▶2.12 **Listen and complete the conversation. Then practise with your partner.**

Waiter: Good *afternoon (evening)*.

Woman: Oh, hello. Can I have some
.... , please?

Waiter: Yes, of course. Would you like a
.... with that?

Woman: No, thank you.

Waiter: And would you like a drink?

Woman: Yes, please. Can I have some
.... ?

Waiter: Sure, no problem.

8 **Have a conversation in a café. Take turns to be the waiter.**

EP Get talking!

Good morning.
Good afternoon.
Good evening.
Would you like a …
Yes, please.
No, thank you.

Maths
Coins and money

1 Look at these coins. Match the coins to the numbers in the box.
You can use two numbers twice.

> 5   10   2   50   1   20

There are 100 pence in a pound.

2 Read, think and choose the correct answer.

1 Peter has got three coins.

The total value is 27 pence. What are the missing coins?

A a two-pence coin and a one-pence coin
B a one-pence coin and a five-pence coin
C a two-pence coin and a five-pence coin

2 Gemma has got three coins.

The total value is 75 pence. What are the missing coins?

A a fifty-pence coin and a ten-pence coin
B a twenty-pence coin and a five-pence coin
C a five-pence coin and a fifty-pence coin

3 Fred has got four coins.

The total value is £2.60 What are the missing coins?

A a two-pence coin, a two-pound coin and a five-pence coin
B a one-pound coin, a fifty-pence coin and a ten-pence coin
C a fifty-pence coin, a twenty-pence coin and a ten-pence coin

3 Do this problem with a partner.

Janet has got five coins. The total value is £1.92. She has got one fifty pence coin. What are the other coins?

a

b

c

d

e

f

g

h

4 Do these sums. Add (+) the money and find the answers.

1 63p + 87p =
2 £1.95 + 32p =
3 £5.45 + £3.64 =
4 98p + £1.15 =

30	thirty
40	forty
50	fifty
60	sixty
70	seventy
80	eighty

Then check with a partner. Take turns to say the sums.

Example   27p + £1.24 = £1.51

> Twenty-seven pence plus one pound twenty-four equals one pound fifty one.

5 Do these sums. Subtract (−) the money and find the answers.

1 37p − 12p =
2 88p − 33p =
3 £5.22 − 46p =
4 £3.99 − £2.50 =

Then check with a partner. Take turns to say the sums.

Example   £1.04p − 16p = 88p

> One pound four pence minus sixteen pence equals eighty-eight pence.

6 **Do these problems with a partner.**

1 The computer game usually costs £25.00. Today it is on sale for £6.01 off the price. How much is it?

2 Mike has got £10.00. He goes to the shops. He buys bananas for 75p, apples for £1.12, milk for 62p and eggs for £2.17. How much money has he got left?

3 Penny wants to buy some shoes. They cost £39.99 and she has got £25.27. Her mum gives her £14.50. How much has she got now? Can she buy the shoes?

4 Three friends want to buy some food for a party. Andrei has got £2.41, Jim has got £3.79 and Suzie has got £4.65. How much have they got altogether?

7 **Do these sums. Multiply (x) or divide (÷) the money and find the answers.**

1 27p x 5 =   4 £2.65 ÷ 5 =
2 65p x 3 =   5 £1.94 ÷ 2 =
3 £1.55 x 8 =   6 £7.26 ÷ 3 =

Check with a partner and say the sums.

37p x 3 = £1.11

> Thirty-seven pence times three equals one pound eleven pence.

£2.16 ÷ 6 = 36p

> Two pounds sixteen pence divided by six equals thirty-six pence.

8 **Do these problems with a partner.**

Menu

Chicken and chips	£6.99
Fish and chips	£5.99
Sandwiches	£3.75
Cakes	£ 3.30
Tea / Coffee / Milk	£1.80
Juice	£2.20

1 The Brown family go to the café. Mr and Mrs Brown have chicken and chips and tea. Sam and Paula have sandwiches. They both have milk to drink. How much is the bill?

2 The Green family go the café. There are four people in the family. Three people have fish and chips and one person has a sandwich. Two people have tea and two people have juice. They all have some cake. How much is the bill?

3 Chris goes to the shop and buys eleven pens. The eleven pens cost £13.31 altogether. All the pens are the same price. How much is each pen?

4 Adam has £20.00. He wants to buy flowers for his mum and chocolate bars for his dad. He buys twelve roses and has £9.20 left. The chocolate bars cost 80p.
   a) How much is each flower?
   b) How many chocolate bars can he buy?
   c) How much money has he got left?

9 **The money in the United Kingdom is called 'pounds and pence'. What is the money called in your country? How many coins are there? What are they?**

10 **Work in pairs. Write some money problems for another pair to answer.**

Project

Find out what the money is called in another English-speaking country. How many coins are there? What are they?

Review 3
Units 9–12

VOCABULARY

1 Write sentences about the pictures.

0 I ___wake up___ at ___quarter to seven___ .
1 I .... at ....
2 I .... at ....
3 I .... at ....
4 I .... at ....
5 I .... at ....
6 I .... at ....

2 Circle the technology words.

som**computer**eugemaildopamemorystickmdinternetsalwebsitejktextftnco

GRAMMAR

3 Put the words in order to make questions. Then ask and answer.

0 your English dad speak Does ?
Does your dad speak English?
1 use Do a you every computer day ?
2 teacher Does your like newspapers reading ?
3 memory stick you a have in bag your Do ?
4 to Do parents your concerts go ?
5 Do get parents you up your before ?

4 Play in pairs: O and X.

Make a correct question and put O or X in the box.

Try to make a line of three Os or Xs.

How much …?	Who …?	What kind of …?
Where …?	How many …?	What time …?
When …?	What …?	How often …?

5 **Ask and answer with a partner. Ask with *How often* and answer with *always, often, sometimes* or *never*.**

A: *How often do you wake up at 5 am?*
B: *I never wake up at 5 am.*

0 wake up at 5 am?
1 sleep until lunchtime?
2 clean the bathroom?
3 eat biscuits in bed?
4 help your friends with their homework?
5 go to bed after 12 o'clock?
6 watch a movie with your parents?

LISTENING

6 ▶2.13 **Listen to the interview. How many questions do you hear?**

Listen again and correct the sentences.

0 Gail lives in London.
  Gail doesn't live in London. She lives …
1 Gail goes to school with her sisters.
2 Gail likes history and geography.
3 Gail sees her friends every day.
4 Gail likes watching sport on TV.

READING

7 **Read the message from a penpal website and answer the questions.**

penpalchatter.com

| HOME | FIND A PENPAL | JOIN PENPALS | CHAT | WHO'S ONLINE | MY ACCOUNT |

Hi everyone,

My name's Sasha and I come from Russia. I'm 14 years old and I go to school in Saint Petersburg. My favourite subjects are maths and science. I love all sports and I play football and basketball for my school.

In my free time I play computer games or go out with my friends. We often go to see a movie and we sometimes go to a café for a drink. I don't watch much TV but I listen to a lot of music. My favourite bands are Radiohead and Muse. I'm learning to play the guitar – it's really good fun!

What about you? What's your name? How old are you? What kind of things do you like doing? Write to me soon!

1 How old is Sasha?
2 Where does he go to school?
3 What are his favourite school subjects?
4 What sports does he do?

5 What does he like doing with his friends?
6 What are his favourite bands?
7 What does Sasha want people to do?

WRITING

8 **Write an email to Sasha. Answer his questions and tell him all about you.**

13 Places
Is there a cinema?

LISTENING

1 Look at the photos and answer the questions. Compare your answers with your partner.

1 Who can you see?
2 Where are they?

▶ 2.14 **Listen and check.**

2 ▶ 2.14 **Listen again. Who says these sentences?**

1 We've got lots of questions for him.
2 We're waiting to take pictures of you.
3 Are there any photographers in the park?
4 I don't want to talk to them.
5 Let's go to my house.
6 This way, José. RUN!

VOCABULARY

3 Look at Rosa's photos for the 'Our town' project. Which places do you know?

OUR TOWN by Rosa

a

b

c

d   CINEMAS

e

f

g

h

4 Look at the word map and at Rosa's photos. Match the photos to the places.

▶2.15 **Listen and repeat.**

5 Complete the sentences with the places in a town.

0 You go to a ....*hotel*........ to sleep the night.
1 You go to .... to study science.
2 You visit a .... to learn about the history of a town.
3 You go to a .... to get some money.
4 You wait at the .... for a train.
5 You meet at the .... and see a film.
6 You go to a .... for a meal.
7 You stay in .... to get better.

Word map:

- museum
- cinema
- hospital
- bank
- **places in a city or town**
- restaurant
- hotel
- university
- station

About you

6 Make a word map of your town. Add other places you know. Then talk to your partner about your town.

There's a swimming pool and a station in my town. There are also some cafés but there aren't any cinemas!

GRAMMAR   *Is there a …? / Are there any …?*

Is there a	photographer cinema university	here?	Yes, there is. No, there isn't.
Are there any	photographers banks museums	in the town? in this street?	Yes, there are. No, there aren't.

→ Grammar reference **page 149**

7 Look at the Grammar box and complete these sentences.

0 ....*Is there a*.... café in this street? No, ...*there isn't*.... .
1 .... cinema in the town? No, ...
2 .... restaurants in this street? Yes, ...
3 .... university here? No, ...
4 .... banks in the town? Yes, ...
5 .... museum here? Yes, ...
6 .... parks in the town? No, ...

▶2.16 **Listen and check.**

SPEAKING

8 Do the activity on page 126.

Is there a restaurant in your town?

Yes, there is.

Where is it?

It's a great place to visit!

My FAVOURITE place

Tell us about your favourite place in 50 words.

I live in Sydney, Australia and my favourite place is the new swimming pool. It's really near the sea. It's big and it's always very clean. I often meet my friends there and we have lots of fun! It's a very safe place to swim. It's beautiful and it's cheap, too!

Karen

I live in London, England and my favourite place is London Zoo. It's exciting to go there but it's expensive! You can see lots of different animals. There are tall animals and very small animals. I like the giraffes best. They're very funny. You can see them from outside!

Robyn

I'm from Rosario, Argentina and my favourite place is a little restaurant below our flat. It's a great place to eat and it's famous for its fish. The food is always good and it's not expensive. I go with my family every weekend. I love living above a restaurant!

Arturo

I'm from Bruges in Belgium and my favourite place is the chocolate factory. Belgium is famous for its chocolate! You can go inside the factory and watch people making the chocolate. It's really interesting. The factory is very important for our town. I want to work there one day.

Jan

READING

1 Look at the photos. What can you see?

2 Read the texts and match them with the photos.

3 Read the texts again and answer the questions.

1 Where does Karen live?
2 Where is the chocolate factory?
3 Which animals does Robyn like?
4 When does Arturo go to the restaurant?

VOCABULARY

4 Find these adjectives in the texts.

> beautiful   cheap   exciting   expensive   great
> important   interesting   little   new   safe   tall

5 Read the example and answer the question.

The factory is very <u>important</u> for our town.
What is very important? ....

Now choose the correct word.

Adjectives tell us more about *nouns / verbs*.

6 Write the opposite of the adjectives. You can find them in Exercise 4.

big	............*little*............
cheap	....
short	....
boring	.... and
	....
OLD	....

GRAMMAR   Prepositions *inside, outside, above, below, near*

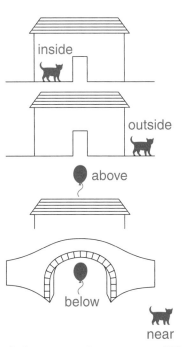

→ Grammar reference **page 149**

7 Look at the picture and complete the sentences with the prepositions.

0 The supermarket is ....*near*........ Jack's flat.
1 Jack's flat is .... the restaurant.
2 Jack is .... his flat.
3 The supermarket is .... the café.
4 There's a car .... the supermarket.
5 The café is .... the supermarket.

8 Make questions. Then ask and answer with your partner.

A: What can you put inside a sandwich?
B: You can put cheese and tomato inside it.

0 What / can / put / inside / sandwich?
1 What / can / see / outside / window?
2 What / got / on / wall / above / bed?
3 there / cinema / near / house?
4 there / exercises / below / this one?

SPEAKING

9 Read the four texts on page 82. Which place do you like best? Why? Tell your partner.

About you

10 Think about your favourite place in your town or city. Use a word map to write some notes about it. Then tell your partner about it.
My favourite place is the new juice bar. It's near the school. All the drinks are very good for you and it isn't expensive.

WRITING

11 Write about your favourite place.
Use adjectives in your writing. They make it interesting to read.

14 Going out
Why are they doing that?

READING AND VOCABULARY

1 Read the story and look at the pictures. Choose the right words to complete the sentences.

▶ 2.17

Picture 1 Jason doesn't want Toby to eat *the pizza* / *the oranges*.

Picture 2 Toby wants to *go swimming* / *eat some food* before his family.

Picture 3 Sally wants *Jason* / *Toby* to swim with her.

Picture 4 The cows *are eating* / *are sitting on* the food.

2 Look at the words in the box. Find these things in the pictures.

> cow   grass   picnic   river   tree

3 Read the story again. Match the sentences with the pictures.

0 Katie is playing in the water and Dad is swimming.   Picture .... 3 .... ☐
1 Toby is taking some pizza.   Picture .... ☐
2 The family are looking at the cows under the tree.   Picture .... ☐
3 Jason is asking Nat and Katie to help.   Picture .... ☐
4 Toby is sitting on the grass and he is pointing.   Picture .... ☐
5 The family are running to the river.   Picture .... ☐

Number the sentences in the order of the story.

GRAMMAR   *Why ...?*   *because*

Katie: Why are the cows sitting on our picnic?

Jason: Because cows always lie down before rain!

The cows are sitting on our picnic because cows always lie down before rain.

→ Grammar reference **page 150**

4 Read the story again. Match the questions to the answers.

1 Why doesn't Katie want to help her mother?   **a** Because he's hungry.
2 Why is Toby taking some pizza?   **b** Because he can see the cows.
3 Why are the family running to the river?   **c** Because she wants to swim.
4 Why is Toby pointing?   **d** Because it's raining.
5 Why are the cows sitting down?   **e** Because they are going swimming.

5 Write sentences with *because*. Then compare your sentences with your partner.

I always walk to school because it's good for me.

		I like her.
I drink lots of milk		I like helping people.
I always walk to school		we don't have a car.
I often help my teacher	because	I like it.
I want to be a doctor		it's good for me.
		I'm good at science.
		she asks me.
		I live in the same street.

6 Write questions for these answers.

0 Because I can't find my pen.
   Why are you writing with a pencil?
1 Because I can't find my phone.
2 Because my favourite film is on at the cinema.
3 Because it's my brother's birthday tomorrow.
4 Because it isn't very interesting.
5 Because I want to watch the football match tonight.
6 Because I don't like walking to school.

SPEAKING AND WRITING

7 Look at picture 1 of the story for one minute. Then close your book. Talk with your partner. What can you remember?

A: I think the cows are behind the tree.

B: Yes, they are and Sally is near the tree. She's taking the drinks out of the box.

8 Write a description of picture 1.

Let's meet at the museum

LISTENING

1 ▶2.18 Anya wants to meet her friends at the weekend. Listen and write the names in her diary.

> Alex   Alexei   Ali   Annie   Benny   Clara   Penny   Sara

	morning	afternoon	evening
Saturday		Meet .... at .... inside the cinema.	Meet .... at .... at the juice bar.
Sunday	Meet .... at .... at the swimming pool.	Meet .... at .... outside the science museum.	

2 ▶2.18 Listen again and write the times in Anya's diary.

3 Talk to people in your class.

Hi, Dan.

Hi, Paula. How are you?

Fine, thanks. And you?

I'm great!

Hi, Lisa.

LEO! How are you doing?

I'm good, thanks. How are you?

I'm fine, thanks.

GRAMMAR   *Let's ..., Shall we ...?*

Let's	meet on Saturday. go to the cinema.	Yes, that's a good idea.
Shall we	visit Bruno? go shopping?	I'd love to. Sorry, I can't ...

→ Grammar reference **page 150**

4 Complete this part of Anya's conversation with Penny. Use the Grammar box to help you.

Anya: (1) .... go swimming on Saturday.

Penny: (2) .... go on Saturday but Sunday morning's OK.

Anya: That's OK for me, too.

Penny: (3) .... meet at the swimming pool?

Anya: (4) .... At quarter to ten?

▶2.19 Listen and check.

5 Practise the conversation in Exercise 4 with your partner. Change the times and places.

VOCABULARY

6 Match 1–5 with a–j. There is more than one answer.

a a museum
b at eight o'clock
1 go
c running
2 go out with
d a famous person
3 go to
e swimming
4 meet
f shopping
5 visit
g friends
h the park
i in the afternoon
j a restaurant

About you

7 Tick (✔) the things in Exercise 6 which you do on Saturday and Sunday. Tell your partner.

SPEAKING

8 Make a diary like Anya's. Look at the adverts and choose two activities. Write the activities and times in your diary.

9 Talk to three friends. Make plans for Saturday and Sunday. See page 127 for an example conversation.

New swimming pool: Big opening!

Free entry this weekend only!

Mario's

Do you like Italian food?
Come and try our pizzas.
We have all your favourites.
Open all day Saturday and Sunday

THIS WEEKEND ONLY
Saturday: 16.00 and 20.00   Sunday: 16.00

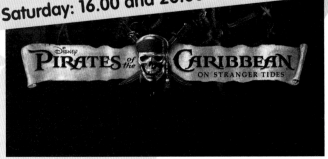

DISNEY
PIRATES of the CARIBBEAN
ON STRANGER TIDES

Rock in the park

Tickets £24

Sunday afternoon at 2pm

Sale

Sale – 50% off
Open Saturday 9–6

Culture
Important places around the world

1 Read the first paragraph and look at pictures A, B, C and D. Can you name these places? What countries are they in?

FAMOUS PLACES

Every country has one or more very special places. These can be buildings, old cities, statues or even mountains. These places are very important to the people of that country. Sometimes the places are famous around the world too.

At Angkor, in Cambodia, there is an ancient stone city. Some of the buildings are about 2,000 years old. Angkor Wat is one of them. It is a very important temple in Cambodia. There is even a picture of it on the Cambodian flag. It has around a million visitors a year.

Machu Picchu is in Peru. It is an Inca city in the Andes mountains and it is 550 years old. There are many buildings there – temples, palaces, houses and gardens. There is also a pyramid. It is a very important place for learning about the Incas. It has about a million visitors a year.

The Taj Mahal is in the city of Agra, in India. It is a very famous and beautiful mausoleum, for a queen called Mumtaz Mahal. About three million people visit it every year. It is 360 years old.

Stonehenge is a very famous monument in the UK. It is an ancient stone circle. People began building it about 5,000 years ago, but even today, we are not sure how, or why it is there. Around 800,000 people a year visit Stonehenge from all over the world.

NEW WORDS

monument – an important building

pyramid –

ancient – very old

temple – some people worship God in this building

mausoleum – this building is for the body of an important person

palace – a very important person lives in this building

statue –

2 Read the texts once to check your answers. Then read them again and complete the table.

	Name of place	Country	Age	Kind of place	Number of visitors	Interesting fact
A		India				
B			5,000 years old			
C	Stonehenge					People don't know why it is there.
D				city		

3 ▶2.20 Match the numbers with the words. Then listen, check and repeat.

a	100	two hundred and fifty
b	250	two million
c	1,000	four hundred thousand
d	3,500	three thousand five hundred
e	400,000	a thousand
f	2,000,000	a hundred

4 Practise saying these numbers with your partner.

440   1,200   650   4,000,000   3,000   6,800   300,000   1,500,000

5 Use the table to make sentences about the places. Your partner must say the name of the place.

This place is 360 years old.   The Taj Mahal.   Yes!

6 Look at the photographs E–H. Do you know these places?

7 Student A, turn to page 127. You have information about places E and F.
Student B turn to page 129. You have information about places G and H.
Ask and answer about the places.

A: What's place E called in English?
B: It's …
A: Is it in Italy?
B: No, it isn't. It's in …

Project

Work in pairs. Choose a famous place from your country, or another country. It can be a building, a statue, a mountain, a bridge, etc.
Write down:
- its name
- its age
- where it is
- what kind of place it is
- one or two interesting facts about it

Use books or the internet to help you. Find a good photograph of the place. Make a poster with your photo and your information. Show it to the class.

15 Clothes
He's wearing José's jacket

LISTENING

1 ▶ **2.21 Listen and choose the right words to complete the sentences.**

1 There are some photographers *outside the house* / *at José's hotel.*
2 Paolo *knows* / *doesn't know* how to help José.
3 Joelle *can find some* / *can't find any* clean clothes in Paolo's bedroom.
4 Paolo *likes* / *doesn't like* wearing José's clothes.
5 José *likes* / *doesn't like* wearing Paolo's clothes.

VOCABULARY

2 ▶ **2.22 Look at the pictures of the clothes. Listen and repeat.**

3 Look at the photos and find the clothes from Exercise 2.

1 dress
2 shoe
3 jeans
4 jacket
5 skirt
6 hat
7 glasses
8 trousers
9 T-shirt
10 shirt
11 watch

About you

4 Ask and answer the questions with your partner.

What do you wear …

- to go to school?
- on a cold day?
- to go out for dinner
- to go to parties?
- on a hot day?

with your family?

GRAMMAR Plurals – spelling

always plural	add -s	add -es	change -y to -ies
clothes	coat → coats	watch → watches	party → parties
jeans	shoe → shoes	dress → dresses	factory → factories
trousers	hotel → hotels	box → boxes	
glasses	cake → cakes		

→ Grammar reference page 151

5 Look at the table in the Grammar box. Write the plural of these words.

0 shirt *shirts*
1 body
2 dictionary
3 skirt
4 waiter
5 address
6 house
7 museum
8 doctor
9 drink
10 cinema
11 sentence
12 sandwich
13 university
14 shop
15 movie

PRONUNCIATION Plurals

6 ▶2.23 Listen and repeat the words in the table.

/s/	/z/	/ɪz/
coats cakes	shoes jeans	watches dresses

7 ▶2.24 Now listen and write the words in the table.

> addresses   cinemas   doctors
> drinks   houses   museums
> sandwiches   sentences   shirts
> shops   skirts   waiters

▶2.25 Listen and check. Then repeat.

SPEAKING AND WRITING

8 Talk about the differences between pictures a and b with your partner.

*A: In picture a, there's one radio and in
  picture b, there are two radios.*
B: Oh yes! You're right!

9 Write about six differences in the pictures.

She's got red hair

VOCABULARY

1 Look at the picture of people at a carnival. Describe the people a–i. Use the words in the box.

> dark hair   short hair   long hair   a brown beard   a red nose   beautiful eyes   big ears
> tall   short   slim   fat   young   old
> a long skirt   a red shirt   a white coat   a red dress   a little hat   red and yellow trousers
> blue trousers

Person a – dark hair, long hair, tall, slim, a long skirt

LISTENING

2 ▶2.26 **Listen to Mike and his friend Frank. They are talking about Mike's carnival photos. Complete the sentences.**

Mike's mum is person ....
Mike's dad is person ....

3 ▶2.26 **Listen again and complete the sentences about Mike's mum and dad.**

0 Mike's mum is ....*tall*........ .
1 Mike's mum is wearing a long blue .... and a white ....
2 She's got long dark ....
3 Mike's dad has got a big red .... and red ....
4 He's wearing red and yellow ....
5 He's wearing very big ....

GRAMMAR Describing people

4 **Complete the table with the words from Exercise 1.**

He/She's (has) got …	He/She's (is) …	He/She's (is) wearing …
long hair	tall	big shoes

→ Grammar reference **page 151**

5 **Look at the 's in these sentences. Write *is* or *has*.**

0 She's tall and beautiful.   ......*is*.......
1 He's wearing my new jeans!   ....
2 She's got lots of shoes.   ....
3 He's very old and he's got grey hair.   ....
4 She's got blue eyes and a small nose.   ....
5 He's wearing a beautiful new watch.   ....

6 **Look at the pictures in Exercise 1 again and describe a person. Your partner says the person.**

A: She's got dark hair and beautiful eyes.
B: Is it person a?

WRITING

7 **Write three sentences about a person in your class. Read your sentences to the class. The class says the person's name.**

This person has got short brown hair. She's tall and slim.
She's wearing jeans.

SPEAKING

8 **You are going to a carnival. Draw a picture of you. You are wearing carnival clothes.**

9 **Work in pairs.**

Student A: Describe your picture to your partner.

Student B: Listen to your partner and draw the picture.

10 **Compare your pictures. Are they the same or different?**

16 Buy it!
We need to go shopping

I want to go to a party with my friends tonight. I need some new clothes.

I want to paint a picture. I need some paint and some paper.

I need to buy some more plates and cups.

Oh dear! Toby needs some new toys!

I need to get some flowers. And the children want to buy some chocolates.

Me!

Me too!

I do!

Who wants to go shopping?

▶2.28

VOCABULARY

1 ▶2.27 **Look at the pictures and find these things. Then listen and repeat.**

clothes   cups   flowers   paint   plates   toys

READING

2 Read the story. Are the sentences right (✔) or wrong (✗)?

1 Nat has got some new clothes.
2 Katie has got lots of paint and paper.
3 Sally likes her cups and plates.
4 Sally wants to buy Toby some new toys.
5 It's Sally's birthday on 20th May.
6 The family want to go shopping.

GRAMMAR   *need, want*

3 Read the story again and think about the difference between *need* and *want*. Then choose the right word to complete these sentences.

> **1** Nat's clothes are old and small. He needs / wants some new clothes.
>
> **2** Nat likes having fun with his friends. He needs / wants to go to the party.

4 Match sentences 1–4 with a–d.

> **1** I want to go to the cinema.   **a** I need some new balls.
>
> **2** I want to do my homework.   **b** I need to go shopping.
>
> **3** I want to play tennis.   **c** I need my books.
>
> **4** I want some new jeans.   **d** I need to buy a ticket.

5 Find all the sentences in the story with *need* and *want*. Then choose the right word to complete these sentences.

> **1** We always / never use *to* with a verb after *need* and *want*.
>
> **2** You can / can't use a noun after *need* and *want*.

→ Grammar reference page 152

6 Complete the sentences with *need* or *want*.

0 This football is old. I ....*need*.... a new ball.

1 My friends are outside. I .... to play football with them.

2 We .... to watch TV. Our favourite film is on tonight.

3 I haven't got any money. I .... to go to the bank.

4 A: Can I go out with my friends?

   B: No, you .... to do your homework.

5 Toby is hungry. He .... some food.

6 Toby isn't hungry but he .... an ice cream.

LISTENING

7 ▶ 2.29 Listen. Which shop do they need?

Conversation 1   **a** toy shop

Conversation 2   **b** music shop

Conversation 3   **c** supermarket

Conversation 4   **d** clothes shop

Conversation 5   **e** bookshop

8 In conversation 1 the girl says *I need to get a new skirt*. Here *get = buy*. Look at these different meanings of *get* and match them to sentences 1–4.

> a give   b buy   c arrive   d catch

1 What time do you **get** home every evening?

2 I need to **get** some new tennis shoes.

3 Let's **get** the bus. I don't want to walk.

4 I'm thirsty, Mum. Can you **get** me a drink?

SPEAKING

9 Ask your partner to do an activity with you. Talk about what you need.

- have a party for your friends
- go to the park
- go to a football match

What do you want to do?

Let's have a party!

OK. What do we need?

We need to get some cakes and …

They're too expensive

READING

1 Read the story and answer the questions.

1 Why does the boy go shopping?
2 Does he buy anything in the shop?

GRAMMAR *too*

2 Match the questions with the answers.

What's wrong with the jeans …
1 in Picture 2?
2 in Picture 3?
3 in Picture 4?
4 in Picture 5?

a They're too expensive.
b They're too big.
c They're too long.
d They're too small.

3 Choose the right word(s).

We use *too* + adjective when something is right / not right.

→ Grammar reference **page 152**

4 Complete the sentences with the words in the box.

> too cold   too difficult   too dirty   too hot
> ~~too short~~

0 He can't go on the ride. He's
...... *too short* ....

1 He can't talk. He's
....

2 He can't walk on the beach.
It's ....

3 She can't do the test. It's
....

4 He can't see out of the
bus. The window is
....

VOCABULARY

5 ▶️ 2.30 Listen and repeat the prices.

6 Work in pairs. Write some prices. Ask your partner to say them.

LISTENING AND SPEAKING

7 ▶️ 2.31 Listen and complete the conversations.

1 £5.25
2 €8.15
3 20p
4 $6.10
5 €16
6 $1.20

1
Can I help you?

How much are these
.... , please?

They're £ ....

Can I have a blue one
and a green one, please?

Of course. That's
£ ....

2
Hi. Can I have a chocolate
.... , please?

Sure. That's $ ....

Thanks.

8 Practise the conversations with a partner.

About you

9 Ask and answer with your partner.
• How often do you go shopping?
• Who do you go shopping with?
• Where do you go shopping?
• Do you enjoy going shopping?
• What's your favourite shop?

Excuse me. How much is this
.... , please?

It's € ....

3
Here you are.

Thanks.

10 Work in pairs. Complete the shopping conversation with your ideas. Act it.

A: Can I help you?
B: I need some/a ....
A: Yes, of course.
B: Sorry. This is / These are too ....
A: OK. Do you like this/these?
B: How much .... ?
A: It's/They're ....
B: Here you are.
A: Thank you.

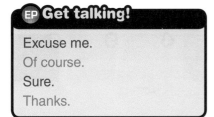

EP Get talking!

Excuse me.
Of course.
Sure.
Thanks.

Music
The orchestra

What is an orchestra?

An orchestra is a large group of people who play music together on different instruments. A modern orchestra can have more than 100 people in it and can make a lot of different kinds of music. Every large orchestra needs a conductor. When the orchestra performs, the conductor stands at the front and leads the musicians. He shows them when the music is fast or slow, loud or quiet.

There are four groups of instruments in an orchestra. These groups are called strings, brass, woodwind and percussion. Many orchestras also have a piano.

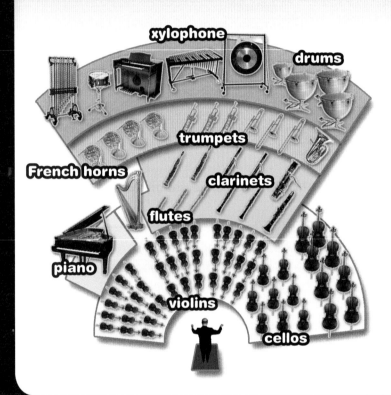

Strings – This very large group sits close to the conductor. You can find instruments like the violins and cellos here. This group of instruments is very important and is sometimes called the heart of the orchestra.

Woodwind – This section is behind the strings section. Some of the instruments in the woodwind section are clarinets, flutes and oboes.

Brass – This part of the orchestra is loud and strong. Examples of instruments in the brass section are trumpets and French horns.

Percussion – These are instruments you hit to make a sound. Drums and xylophones are part of this group but there are lots of other kinds of percussion instruments, too.

The Simon Bolivar Orchestra

1 Read the text and match the parts of the orchestra diagram with the correct colour.

brass   conductor   percussion   piano
strings   woodwind

1   **2**   **3**   **4**   **5**   **6**

2 ▶2.32 **Listen. Which part of the orchestra is playing?**

1 ....
2 ....
3 ....
4 ....
5 ....

3 **Work in pairs. Read the text and look at the pictures. How often do you think you listen to orchestra music? Tell your partner.**

Is that an orchestra?

How often do you listen to orchestra music? Is your answer 'never'? Well, think again! Do you watch movies? Do you play computer games? Do you go to shopping centres? Do you watch TV shows and adverts on TV? All of these use orchestral music. This is because orchestral music is very good at changing how you feel. It can make you feel happy, sad, excited or scared.

a

b

c

d

4 ▶2.33 **Listen to a piece of music and answer the questions.**

1 Is the music fast or slow?
2 Which parts of the orchestra can you hear?
3 How does the music make you feel?
4 Which picture do you think matches this music?

Project

Find some orchestra music on the internet and listen to it.
- Complete the fact file about the music.
- Play your music to the class and talk about it using your fact file.

Fact file	
The name of the music	
The name of the orchestra	
The name of the conductor	
The instruments I can hear	
Some adjectives to describe this music	

Review 4
Units 13–16

VOCABULARY

1 What can you see in
the picture? Talk about
it with your partner.
How many sentences
can you make?

A: *Some people are*
   walking in the street.
B: *Yes, and there are*
   some tall buildings.

2 Label the things in the bedroom.

3 What are you wearing?
Stand with your back to your partner.
Say what he or she is wearing.

You're wearing a
yellow T-shirt and
trousers. I think your
trousers are light blue.

You're wearing …

GRAMMAR

4 Write the plurals of these words. Put a tick
(✔) in the box to show the spelling rule.

			-s	-es	-ies
0	plate	plates	✔		
1	dollar				
2	city				
3	watch				
4	cow				
5	cup				
6	river				
7	sandwich				
8	picnic				
9	nationality				

5 Complete the sentences with *want* or *need*.

0 I haven't got a coat. I ....*need*.... to buy one.

1 That film is interesting. I .... to go and see it.

2 My hands are dirty. I .... to wash them.

3 I can't find my English book. I .... to get a new one.

4 The river is beautiful. I .... to go swimming.

5 José is a famous singer. I .... to meet him.

6 We've got a test tomorrow. I .... to do my homework now.

LISTENING

6 ▶2.34 **Listen to the conversation. Write the prices on the menu.**

River Café MENU

food

Vegetable soup and bread	£4.10
Fish with rice or potatoes	£ ....
Pasta with tomato sauce	£5.15
Chicken and chips	£ ....
Pizza	£5.00
Ice cream	£ ....

drinks

Tea	£2.00
Coffee	£ ....
Orange juice	£ ....
Apple juice	£ ....
Water	£1.00

SPEAKING

7 **You are going on a picnic. Make a list with your partner of things you want to buy.**

> Let's get some cheese.

> Good idea. Shall we buy some bread, too?

READING

8 **Read the notes. Complete them with the words from the box.**

> buy   go   meet   visit

Mike

.... me at the new café at 5.30. I haven't got my mobile!

Susie

Tina

Your sandwiches are on the table. I've got to .... your dad in hospital!

Mum

Daniela

There's no fish food! Please .... some from the shop.

Dad

Louis

Shall we .... shopping later? Wait for me!

Sasha

9 **Read the sentences. Write *yes* or *no*.**

0 Louis is at the shops now.   no

1 The fish need some food.

2 There's some food for Tina in the kitchen.

3 Sasha wants Louis to wait for him.

4 Mike can send Susie a text.

5 Tina's dad is in hospital.

6 Daniela's dad wants her to buy something.

WRITING

10 **Write a note for your mum or dad. You can choose what to write about.**

17 Comparing
José's house is newer!

LISTENING AND VOCABULARY

1 ▶2.35 **Listen to Part 1 and answer the questions.**

1 Where's José?
2 Where are the photographers? Why?
3 What does José invite Paolo to do?

2 ▶2.36 **Listen to Part 2. Write *yes* or *no*. Then change the *no* sentences to make them true.**

0 The friends are in José's house.
 No. The friends are in José's hotel room.
1 Rosa wants to look at photos of José's family.
2 José's house is in the city.
3 José gives the friends some tickets for his concert.
4 The concert is tomorrow evening.
5 Paolo needs to wash some clothes.

3 **Look at photos a and b. Tick (✔) José's house.**

▶2.36 **Listen to Part 2 again and check.**

GRAMMAR Comparatives: short adjectives

José's house is newer than my house.

My house is older than José's house.

4 Look at the examples.

adjective	comparative	spelling
new	newer than	+ er
old	older than	+ er
small	smaller than	+ er
nice	nicer than	+ r
big	bigger than	double letter + er
dirty	dirtier than	y → i + er

→ Grammar reference **page 153**

Put the comparative form of these adjectives in the right column: *fat*, *tall*, *long*, *hungry*, *safe*, *sad*, *clean*, *hot*, *happy*, *young*, *easy*, *late*

+ er	+ r	double letter + er	y → i + er
		fatter	

5 Complete the sentences. Use the adjectives in the box in the comparative form.

cold   easy   hot   ~~long~~   nice   old   young

0 Lisa's hair is ....*longer than*.... Dora's hair.

1 Winter is .... summer.

2 I love apples. They're .... oranges.

3 English is .... French. I'm not very good at French.

4 I'm .... my sister. She's 15 and I'm 12.

5 But I'm .... my brother. He's only two.

6 India is .... Canada.

PRONUNCIATION *than*

6 ▶ **2.37 Listen and repeat.**

1 Rosa's house is older than José's house.

2 The sea in Brazil is warmer than the sea in England.

About you

7 Compare your home with the photos of houses in Exercise 3. Make sentences, then tell your partner.

SPEAKING AND WRITING

8 Talk about the picture on page 128 with your partner. Use comparatives and the words in the box.

The red car is newer and nicer than the blue one.

This bird is smaller than the baby.

big   clean   cold   dirty   fast   happy   hot
long   new   nice   old   sad   short   slow
small   tall   young

9 Write eight sentences about the picture on page 128.

The boy with the ice cream is happier than the girl with the ice cream.

This is more exciting!

GREAT DAYS OUT

★ **The Eden Project is really interesting.** ★ Gemma 14

The Eden Project

Come and have a fantastic family day out.

See our:
- huge biomes
- wonderful flowers from around the world
- beautiful buildings
- a real rainforest … and more.

There's always lots to do and see. We're open all year round. Look at the website for prices and times.

www.edenproject.com

Alton Towers

We are the best place for an exciting family day out.

We've got:
- a theme park
- a water park
- exciting new rides
- lots of activities … and more.

There are always new rides to go on. We're open from March to November. Look at the website for prices and times.

www.altontowers.com

Woburn Safari Park

Come and have a family day out with us.

You can:
- help at feeding time
- go on a road safari around the park
- learn about all the wild animals
- climb the trees … and more.

There are always new animals to see. We're open every day in the summer and at weekends in the winter. Look at the website for prices and times.

www.woburn.co.uk/safari

Warwick Castle

Visit a beautiful old English castle.

Come and:
- walk around the outside
- visit the rooms inside the castle
- learn about the history of the castle
- listen to scary stories … and more.

There are always new things to do. You won't be bored at Warwick Castle!
We're open every day except Christmas Day. Look at the website for prices and times.

www.warwick-castle.co.uk

★ **Warwick Castle is never boring!** ★ Chris 16

READING AND VOCABULARY

1 **Read about the four days out for the family and answer the questions.**

Where can you …
1 go on a road safari?
2 listen to stories?
3 go on exciting rides?
4 see a rainforest?

2 **Read about the days out again and answer the questions.**

1 Which places can you visit in the winter?
2 Where can you feed animals?
3 Where can you visit a water park?
4 Where are there wonderful gardens?
5 Where can you learn some history?

3 **Read about four families. Choose the best day out for each family.**
Then compare your answers with your partner.

I think the Eden Project is the best place for the Patel family because …

Manesh Patel is a doctor and his wife, Jameela, is a teacher. They haven't got any children. Manesh likes animals and history but Jameela thinks flowers are more interesting than animals.

The Edwards family are from a small village in Wales. Caroline works in a hospital and the twins, Clara and Jack, are 10. They think history is boring, but Caroline loves it. She also likes gardens.

The Baluchi family live in Harrogate, a town in the north of England. Jamal works in a bank and Naima works in a shop. Their son Rafi is 6. He loves animals and thinks safaris are very exciting.

The Nowak family are on holiday in the UK. Jacek is a bus driver and he's got three children: Dobry, who's 8, Lech, who's 12, and Ewa, who's 15. Jacek likes visiting old castles. The children want to do something more exciting and to have fun.

GRAMMAR Comparatives: long adjectives

Warwick Castle is more beautiful than Alton Towers.
Alton Towers is more exciting than Warwick Castle.

→ Grammar reference **page 153**

4 **Write sentences. Use the grammar box to help you.**

0 Houses / expensive / cars.
   Houses are more expensive than cars.
1 The president of the USA / famous / my mum!
2 Science / interesting / maths.
3 Your sister's dress / beautiful / my dress.
4 Tennis / exciting / football.
5 My birthday / important / my brother's birthday.

5 **Make sentences with words from Box A and adjectives from Box B or use your own ideas. Make some sentences true and some not true.**

Box A	Box B
computers Edinburgh	difficult
English geography	exciting
history London maths	expensive
mobiles my dad	famous
my sister my teacher	fun
New York school Sydney	important
the beach the park	interesting

I think maths is more difficult than English.

6 **Read your partner's sentences. Tick (✔) the sentences which you think are true. Then compare answers with your partner.**

About you

7 Think of places for a family day out in your country. Tell your partner about the places you want to visit and why.
A: *I want to visit the Lenfilm Studios. I love films and they make lots of movies there.*
B: *I think animals and wildlife are more interesting than films. I want to go to Tayrona National Park.*

WRITING

8 **Choose one place you want to visit. Describe it and say why you want to go there.**

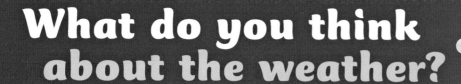

18 The weather
I like it when it's hot!

What do you think about the weather?

Some people love talking about the weather. What about you? Send us a message. Answer one of these questions.

1 How do you feel when it's raining?
2 What sports do you do in the winter?
3 Do you like summer more than winter?

Hannah, 11, Oxford

I play football every winter in the rain and wind and snow. The cold weather doesn't stop me!

Kellie, 13, Southampton

I feel bad when it rains in the holidays. I like doing things outside. I don't want to stay inside reading or watching TV. And you can't go to the cinema every day – it's too expensive.

Libby, 12, Newport

I love sports but it's harder to do them outside in the winter. I play tennis in the summer but not in winter. I often go swimming with my friends on Saturdays in the winter.

Josh, 12, Aberdeen

Rain is just water – it's not a problem. I put on a coat and I go outside and have fun!

David, 13, Suffolk

I have a horse and I ride it every day – in the winter and in the summer. Cold weather's not a problem but we don't like the wind! It's not nice!

Emzi, 11, London

No, I don't like hot sun at all – my favourite kind of weather is snow. It's much more fun to play in.

Finn, 10, Hull

Sad! I want to go on a day out with my parents and my brother but we can't go because it's raining.

Sarah, 14, Derby

Of course! I love the sun. It's my favourite kind of weather. I feel happier when it's warm.

VOCABULARY

1 ▶2.38 Match the pictures to the words. Then listen and repeat.

cold hot rain snow summer sun
warm wind winter

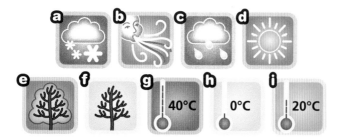

READING

2 Read the messages and match them to the questions on the website.

3 Read the messages on the website again. Who says this?

1 I like the snow more than the sun.
2 It's not easy to do sports in winter.
3 I don't stay inside when it's raining.
4 I can't go out today because of the weather.
5 I like being outside, but not in the rain.
6 Warm weather is better than cold weather.

PRONUNCIATION Vowel sounds

4 Match the words with the same vowel sound.

A	B
snow	stay
wind	sport
rain	love
warm	where
fun	ride
find	coat
watch	stop
wear	live

▶ **2.39** Listen and check. Then repeat.

About you

5 Tell your partner how you feel about the weather.

I love	winter / summer	
I like	cold / warm weather	because …
I don't like	rain / wind	

Yes, me too.
Really? I don't!

GRAMMAR *it*

We can use *it* to talk about the weather.
It's cold today.
I feel happier when it's warm.

Look at how we use *it* in these sentences.

I like tennis but I don't play it in the winter.

You can't go to the cinema every day – it's too expensive.

→ Grammar reference **page 154**

6 Read the website again and find all the examples of *it*.

7 Put the words in the right order to complete the sentences.

0 really / It's / outside / hot
It's really hot outside – let's go to the beach.

1 play / It's / to / fun
.... in the snow.

2 hot / when / good / it's
I don't feel ....

3 it's / but / really / hard
I like maths ....

4 wear / it / you / can
That's my hat but ....

5 but / it / I / play / can't
I've got a guitar ....

SPEAKING

8 Look at the questionnaire. Add three more questions. Then ask and answer with your partner.

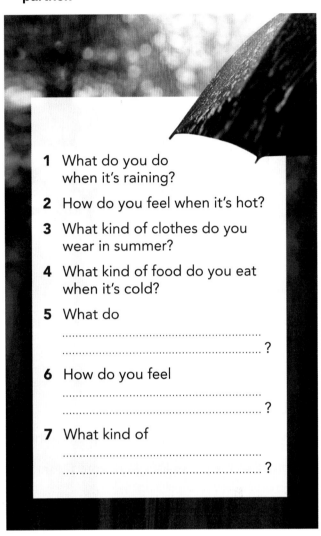

1 What do you do when it's raining?

2 How do you feel when it's hot?

3 What kind of clothes do you wear in summer?

4 What kind of food do you eat when it's cold?

5 What do
....
.... ?

6 How do you feel
....
.... ?

7 What kind of
....
.... ?

9 Tell the class about your partner.

Eva stays at home when it rains. She loves it when it's hot. She likes to eat soup and bread when it's cold.

WRITING

10 Choose a question from the website and write a message about you.

On holiday with my friend

VOCABULARY

1 Look at the pictures and find these things.

> beach   cows   cups   dog   family   farm   plates   rain   sea   sheep   sun   tent

READING

2 Read the postcards and match them with the pictures.

3 Complete the postcards with words from Exercise 1.

Dear Jill,
We are staying on a
(1) ....**farm**........ for the weekend.
The weather's great – it's warm
but it's not too hot. There are
lots of animals here – about 20
(2) ...., 10 cows and a
(3) .... Toby is having
lots of fun.
From Sally and Jason

Hi Paul,
I'm camping for two days with
some of my friends. The weather's
really bad. It's raining and it's cold.
We are all sitting inside the
(4) .... We are staying
here until Friday but we want to go
home today. How is your holiday?
Write soon and tell me.
From Nat

4 Read the postcards again and answer the questions.

1 Does Toby like the farm?
2 What kind of animals are on the farm?
3 Who is Nat camping with?
4 Why does Nat want to go home?
5 Is Katie happy about the weather?
6 How long does Katie stay at the beach every day?
7 Who do you think is having the best holiday?

Dear Jenna,
I'm on holiday with my friend
Sue and her (5) ....
We're here for a week. The
weather is great – it's really
hot and sunny. We go to the
(6) .... every day for
about eight hours. We stay until
the sun goes down. I'm having a
great holiday!
Love Katie

5 Complete the sentences with information about you. Then compare your answers with your partner.

1 The best place for a holiday in my country is ....

2 The best time to go on holiday in my country is ....

3 The best people to go on holiday with are ....

4 Fun things to do on holiday are ....

GRAMMAR Prepositions *with*, *for*, *until*

I'm with Sue.

We're staying here for three days.

We're here until Friday.

→ Grammar reference **page 154**

6 Find examples of *with*, *for* and *until* in the postcards.

7 Complete the sentences with *for*, *with* and *until*.

1 Sam and I are going to Tom's party. Do you want to come .... us?

2 I play football .... about two hours every Saturday.

3 My music lesson doesn't finish .... three o'clock.

4 I can come to the park .... an hour this afternoon.

5 I want to go on holiday .... my friend this year.

6 You can stay at my house .... Saturday.

LISTENING

8 ▶ 2.40 Listen to the conversations and read the questions. Tick (✔) the right picture.

1 What's the boy doing?

Ⓐ   Ⓑ   Ⓒ

2 What time can Pedro and Nat meet at the park?

Ⓐ   Ⓑ   Ⓒ

3 What does Donna need to take on holiday?

Ⓐ   Ⓑ   Ⓒ

4 What kind of animals are on the farm?

Ⓐ   Ⓑ   Ⓒ

WRITING

9 You are on holiday in one of the places in the photos. Write a postcard to a friend. Then read your postcard to the class.

Culture
Canada and the maple tree

1 What do you know about Canada? Talk with your partner. Write down five things you know or would like to know.

2 Now read the text about Canada to check your ideas.

Canada is in North America and is the world's second largest country. Canada is famous for its mountains, lakes and forests, and for its very cold winters.

The Canadian flag is red and white and in the centre there is a maple leaf. The maple leaf is the symbol of Canada. In autumn the leaves of the maple trees change from green to red and yellow and they make the forests look very beautiful.

You can see the maple leaf on a coin, too. Gold maple-leaf coins are made from pure gold and are very expensive.

Canadians use maple trees for many things. Wooden houses are popular in Canada and some people build their houses from maple wood. You can see beautiful tables and chairs made from maple wood in many people's homes.

Perhaps the most famous product of the maple tree is maple syrup. It is very sweet, and people all over the world like to eat Canadian maple syrup on their pancakes and ice cream.

North America

ALASKA

CANADA

USA

3 Read the text again. Complete the phrases below the pictures using the words in the box.

coins   flag   maple x2   syrup

1 the Canadian ....

2 .... furniture

3 maple ....

4 .... leaves

5 gold maple-leaf ....

Making maple syrup

Maple syrup comes from the sap of the maple tree. Sap is the liquid inside the tree. At the end of winter, people put taps into the maple trees. They put more taps into bigger, older trees. The sap runs out of the taps into buckets. People empty the buckets every evening. After about four weeks, people take the taps out of the trees. Each tap produces about forty-five litres of sap in a year. The taps do not hurt the trees and maple trees can live for about thirty years.

People boil the sap to make maple syrup. They boil it for a long time. You need forty litres of maple sap to make one litre of maple syrup!

a ☐ Buckets collect the sap.

b ☐ They boil the sap.

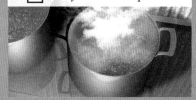

c ☐ A maple tree in winter

d ☐ They put a tap into a maple tree.

e ☐ A litre of maple syrup

f ☐ The sap runs from the tap.

4 Read the text and number the pictures in the right order.

5 Read the text again and answer the questions.

1 Where does maple syrup come from?
2 What time of year do people collect the sap from maple trees?
3 How do people get the sap out of the trees?
4 How much sap comes out of a tap each year?
5 How long can maple trees live?
6 How much sap do you need to make four litres of maple syrup?

6 ▶2.41 Listen to Jessica talking about maple syrup. Put a tick (✔) for the foods she likes to eat with maple syrup. Put a cross (✗) for the foods she doesn't like to eat with maple syrup.

ice cream	bananas	pancakes	bread	toast	meat	fish	cake

Project

Canada is famous for its maple syrup.
What food or drink is your country famous for?
Work with a partner.
Find out where the food or drink comes from.

Find out how people like to eat or drink it.
Find a recipe using the special food or drink.
Make a poster with all your information.
Show it to the class.

19 Going places
We were at a concert

a ☐

We're going home in the ...., ... but happy!

b ☐

Rosa is waiting for the ....

c ☐

José da Silva and his ....

d ☐

These are our .... !

e ☐

With the band at the .... of the concert.

f ☐

Paolo doesn't want to be ....

LISTENING AND VOCABULARY

1 ▶2.42 **Listen and number the photos in the right order.**

2 **Complete the descriptions of each photo with a word from the box.**

> band   bus   car   late   tickets   end   tired

GRAMMAR   Past simple: *be*

3 **Look at the examples from the recording and answer the questions.**

➕	➖	❓	
I was late.	Paolo wasn't there.	Were you tired?	Yes, we were.
It was fantastic!	We weren't late.	Was the music good?	Yes, it was.
We were really excited.			
They were really nice.		Where were you?	

→ Grammar reference **page 155**

Are Paolo, Rosa and Joelle talking about *last night* or *every night*?

Do we use *was* and *were* to talk about *now* or *the past*?

4 **Look at the examples and complete the table with *was, wasn't, were* and *weren't*.**

	I / he / she / it was / wasn't		you / we / they were / weren't	
➕	I .... happy. She .... tall.		You .... late. They .... good.	
➖	I .... tired. It .... in my bag.		You .... at school. We .... cold.	
❓	.... she nice? .... it interesting? Where .... it?	Yes, she .... No, it	.... they good? .... you bored? Where .... your friends?	Yes, they .... No, we ....

5 ▶2.42 **Listen to Joelle, Paolo and Rosa again. Correct the sentences.**

0 Paolo, Joelle and Rosa were at the concert last week.

  They weren't at the concert last week.
  They were at the concert last night.

1 Rosa was late for the bus.

2 The bus was very fast.

3 The concert was at nine o'clock.

4 It was easy to take a photo of the band.

5 Paolo, Joelle and Rosa were tired before the concert.

PRONUNCIATION   *was*

6 ▶2.43 **Listen and repeat.**

A: *Where were you on Saturday afternoon?*
B: *I was at a birthday party.*
A: *Was it fun?*
B: *Yes, it was.*

About you

7 Write five questions. Begin *Where were you …?* Use the ideas below or your ideas. Then ask and answer with your partner.

> yesterday
> last night / last week / last Sunday
> in the morning / on Monday afternoon
> on Friday / on June 1st

> picnic   dance class
> tennis lesson   a maths test
> at home

> interesting   boring   easy
> difficult   exciting   fun

VOCABULARY

1 Put the words in the box in the right column.

> ~~boat~~ bus car ~~computer~~ ~~hat~~ knife
> money notebook plane shoes T-shirt
> tent train trousers water bottle

Ways to travel	Things to wear	Things to take
boat	hat	computer

▶ 2.44 Listen and check. Then repeat. Can you add any words to the table?

READING

Michael Fay has an exciting job. He's an explorer and a scientist, and he travels around the world learning about the plants and animals in different countries. Here, he tells us about his life, and about getting too close to an elephant!

A ....

I think I was a problem for my teachers and my parents because I was only happy when I was outside. One day, when I was about eight, I was in a guitar lesson and I was really bored. I remember thinking 'Why am I sitting inside on a Saturday?' After that there were no more guitar lessons!

B ....

His name was Mr Royce and he was my science teacher when I was eleven. His lessons were great. They were often outside and they were always really interesting.

C ....

I walk! I find plants and animals and write about them in my notebook. I also fly a lot. I've got a small plane and I use that in Africa when I'm working with the elephants. I sometimes need to use a boat as well.

D ....

Some really good shoes, because I walk a lot. Last year, I was in Africa for four months. It was summer there and it was really hot. In my bag there were shoes, a tent, some trousers, a T-shirt, a knife and, of course, my computer. Oh, and there were lots of notebooks!

E ....

Well, I work with elephants and it's important not to get too close to them. I was in Gabon in Central Africa, in 2003. One day, I was in the wrong place and an elephant was not happy to see me. I was in hospital for a few days after that. I don't go too close to elephants now!

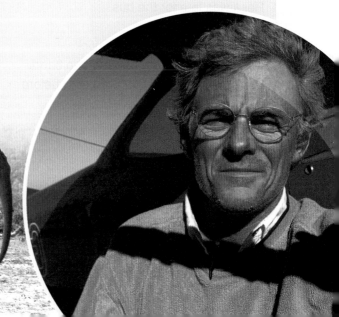

2 Read the first part of the article and look at the photos. Answer the questions.

1 What does Michael Fay do?
2 How do you think Michael Fay travels when he is working?
3 What do you think Michael Fay puts in his bag when he travels?

3 Read the interview with Michael Fay. Check your answers to Exercise 2.

4 Match the questions to the paragraphs in the interview.

1 Who was your favourite teacher?
2 What do you always take with you when you travel?
3 How do you travel?
4 What kind of child were you?
5 How dangerous is your job?

5 Read the interview again and match the questions to the answers.

1 Where was Michael last year?
2 Why wasn't Michael happy in the guitar lesson?
3 How long was Michael's trip to Africa last year?
4 How hot was it in Africa last year?
5 When was Michael in Gabon?
6 Why wasn't the elephant happy to see Michael?

a It was very hot.
b He was too close to it.
c He was in Africa.
d Four months.
e In 2003.
f He was bored.

GRAMMAR   *Wh-* questions in the present and past

6 Read the questions in Exercises 4 and 5 again. Complete the list of question words.

How?   What?   What kind of?   Who?   ....

→ Grammar reference **page 155**

7 Now read the questions again and complete this sentence with *can* or *can't*.

You .... answer these questions with *Yes* or *No*.

8 Put the words in order to make questions. Start each question with a question word.

0 How / in / old / were / 2010 / you / ?
   How old were you in 2010?
1 What / your / is / English / name / teacher's / ?
2 Who / was / student / best / the / today / ?
3 How / your / last / long / was / holiday / ?
4 Where / Saturday / were / you / on / ?
5 What / you / do / school / after / do / ?
6 How / this / was / difficult / exercise / ?

9 Ask and answer the questions with your partner.

About you

10 Work with a partner. Write five questions in the present or past. Use the prompts to help you. Then ask your teacher the questions.
   • What colour / first car?
   • What / put in your bag when you travel?
   • Where / you in 2001?
   • What / favourite book when you / young?
   • How / travel to school every day?

20 A Russian tale
The old man helped Ivan

The Flying Boat – Part 1

Ivan was a poor man. He lived in a small village with his mother. She loved him very much because he was kind. One day, there was a poster on a wall in his village. It said:

WANTED
The BEST husband in the world!
Make me a flying boat and you can be my husband.
Natasha
Daughter of the KING

Ivan was very excited. He wanted to make a flying boat for Natasha. He walked into the forest to eat his lunch and to think. An old man walked up to him and said, 'I'm hungry. Have you got any food for me?' 'Of course,' said Ivan. 'Here you are.' 'Thank you,' the old man said. 'You are very kind.'
'But I'm not clever,' said Ivan, 'and I want to make a flying boat. Can you help me?' 'Yes,' said the old man. 'I can.'

They worked together and very soon they finished the flying boat. It was beautiful. 'Please come with me on the flying boat,' said Ivan.
'I'd love to,' said the old man. 'But listen. This is very important. When we travel to meet the king, invite all the people you see onto your flying boat.'

VOCABULARY AND READING

1 **Find these things in the pictures.**

a bird   a flying boat   a poor family
a poster   trees

2 ▶2.45 **Here are people from the story. Read and listen and match the people to the pictures.**

an old man   Eat-it-all   Ivan   Ivan's mother
Longlegs   See-it-all

3 **Are these sentences right or wrong? Correct the wrong sentences.**

0 Ivan's got a lot of money.
   No. Ivan hasn't got a lot of money.
1 Ivan is clever.
2 Natasha wants a plane.
3 Ivan gives the old man some money.
4 Longlegs is running on the road.
5 See-it-all can see all the birds in the world.
6 Eat-it-all wants some bread for breakfast.

4

'Look, there's a man. He's walking on his hands.' 'Hey,' Ivan said. 'Why are you walking on your hands?' 'Because, when I walk on my long legs, I can go to the other end of the world and I don't want to go there at the moment. My name's Longlegs.'

Ivan invited Longlegs to come on the boat with them.

5

'Look, there's a woman. What's she looking at?'

'Hey, what are you doing?' asked Ivan.

'I'm looking at a bird in a tree at the other end of the world. I can see all the things in the world. My name's See-it-all.'

Ivan invited See-it-all to come on the boat with them.

6

'Look, there's a man. He's carrying a big bag of bread.'

'Hey,' Ivan said. 'What are you doing?'

'I'm going to get some more bread for my dinner. I'm always hungry. I can eat all the bread in the world and I want to eat more. My name's Eat-it-all.'

Ivan invited Eat-it-all to come on the boat with them.

7

So the five people travelled in the flying boat to see the King.

GRAMMAR   Past simple ➕

> The old man wanted to help him.
> We can say:
> I / you / he / she / we / they wanted to help him.

→ Grammar reference **page 156**

4 **Find the past of these verbs in the story.**

> invite   live   love   ~~travel~~   walk   want   work

5 **Complete the sentences with the verbs in Exercise 4 in the past simple.**

0 Last year I ......*travelled*...... to the USA by boat.

1 She .... in a city when she was a child.

2 I .... to school yesterday.

3 We .... on our project last Monday.

4 My friend .... me to her party.

5 He .... his brother very much.

6 I .... to be an explorer when I was a child.

The King didn't like Ivan

The Flying Boat – Part 2

a ☐

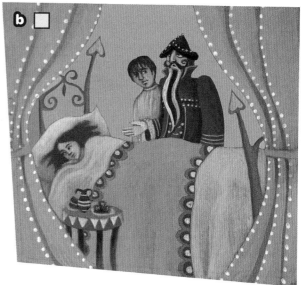

b ☐

c ☐

LISTENING

1 Look at the pictures. Find Natasha and her father, the King.

2 ▶2.46 Number the pictures in the right order. Then listen to Part 2 of the story and check.

3 ▶2.46 Listen again. Match the beginnings of the sentences with the endings.

Picture 1: The King didn't want this man   a   to die.
Picture 2: Now can he   b   to be his daughter's husband.
Picture 3: She wanted   c   and be happy.
Picture 4: Longlegs walked across the world   d   be my husband?
Picture 5: He is   e   a kind man.
Picture 6: Let's all live here together   f   on his long legs.

GRAMMAR   Past simple ⊖

> The King didn't (did not) want Natasha to die.
> We can say:
> I / you / he / she / we / they didn't want Natasha to die.

→ Grammar reference **page 156**

4 Write the negative of these verbs.

0 wanted *didn't want*   6 loved
1 answered   7 started
2 asked   8 travelled
3 died   9 walked
4 finished   10 wanted
5 lived   11 worked

▶2.47 Listen and check. Then repeat.

d

e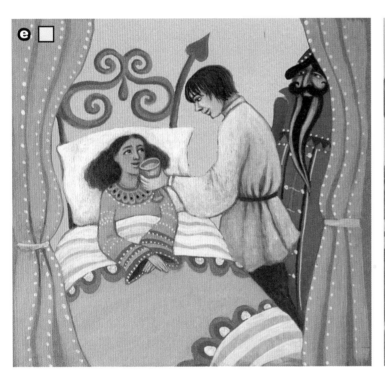

f

5 Correct these sentences about the story.

0 Ivan lived in a town.
  Ivan didn't live in a town. He lived in a village.
1 Ivan wanted to make a toy boat.
2 The five friends travelled by train to see the King.
3 The King asked Ivan to do five things.
4 Natasha loved Eat-it-all.
5 Ivan loved See-it-all.
6 The King was sad at the end of the story.

SPEAKING

6 Work in groups of five. Read the end of the story on page 127. Act it for the class.

WRITING

7 Write a different end for the story. Start with the sentence:

'Ivan can never be your husband,' the King said. 'He is poor and he isn't clever.'

8 In groups of four, read the end of each other's stories. Which do you like best? Why?

About you

9 Think of a traditional story from your country. Tell the story to your group. Then tell them why you like it.

Art
Drawing and perspective

a

The Harbour by Alfred Wallis

Perspective in ART

b

Paris Street: A Rainy Day by Gustave Caillebotte

When we look at the world, we see everything in three dimensions. So, things that are further away from us look smaller than they are. Lines also look like they get closer together as they reach the horizon. This is called perspective.

Look at this photograph of railway lines. We know that railway lines are parallel but in the photo they seem to get closer together in the far distance. The trees in the distance look smaller too but they are really the same size as the ones in the foreground. Your eye follows the railway lines to the place on the horizon where the lines meet. This place is called the vanishing point.

in the distance

horizon

foreground

When we want a painting or drawing to look realistic, we need to make it three-dimensional. We do this by using perspective in our pictures.

1 Work in pairs. Look at the two paintings. Ask and answer these questions with your partner.

1 Which painting looks realistic, like a photo?
2 Which painting looks flat?
3 Do you know why this is?

2 Read the article about perspective. Which painting is an example of three-dimensional perspective?

Relativity by M.C. Escher

Vincent's Bedroom in Arles by Vincent Van Gogh

3 Work in pairs and answer the questions.

Picture c

1 Which stairs go up and which stairs go down?
2 Where is the garden?
3 How many people are walking upstairs?
4 How many vanishing points can you find in the picture?

Picture d

1 Which looks bigger: the chair on the left or the chair next to the bed?
2 Why do some of the pictures on the wall look strange?
3 Is the vanishing point in the picture or beyond it?

Project

Follow these instructions to draw or paint a picture.

1 Use a ruler and a pencil. Draw the horizon. Mark the vanishing point. Draw a road.

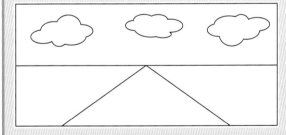

2 Draw a line down the centre of the road and a pavement on the right. Draw a line parallel to the road on the left.

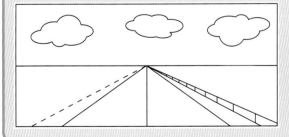

3 Draw some houses on the left. Erase the pencil line.

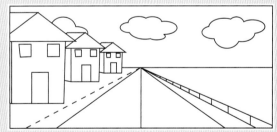

4 Draw some people on the pavement. Draw some more things in your picture, for example trees, clouds, animals.

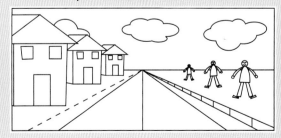

Review 5
Units 17–20

LISTENING

1 ▶2.48 **Gavin travelled to a lot of places this year. What was the weather like? Listen and draw a line.**

January	February	March	April	May	June
wind ✂	cold ❄ ✏	rain ☁	hot ☀	warm ☀	wind ✂
rain ☁	warm ☀	hot ☀	wind ✂	rain ☁	cold ❄
warm ☀	hot ☀	cold ❄	warm ☀	wind ✂	rain ☁
hot ☀	wind ✂	warm ☀	rain ☁	cold ❄	hot ☀
cold ❄	rain ☁	wind ✂	cold ❄	hot ☀	warm ☀
warm ☀	hot ☀	wind ✂	cold ❄	snow ☁	rain ☁

VOCABULARY

2 Complete the sentences with a word from the box.

> carry cat garden ~~sea~~ show train village

0 I love swimming in the .....sea..... on holiday.

1 Our .... doesn't come with us on holiday. It goes to a kind of animal hotel.

2 Yesterday, I walked to the station to catch the ....

3 You have some beautiful flowers in your ....

4 Can you .... me your new computer game?

5 A .... is smaller than a town.

6 Shall I .... your books for you?

3 Complete the words.

0 A person who doesn't have a lot of money is p.oor........... .

1 In the summer, we sometimes go on a d................. o................. to a zoo.

2 I like to go by f................. train. It's fun and exciting.

3 Last year we travelled by car but it was very s................. .

4 My brother likes playing on the b................. because he can't swim.

5 There are a lot of sheep on my uncle's f................. .

6 I've got two t................. for the concert.

GRAMMAR

4 Make sentences with adjectives from the box. There is more than one answer.

> big clean cold dirty easy exciting
> expensive famous important
> interesting ~~nice~~ old young

0 apples / chocolate
Apples are nicer than chocolate.

1 your school bag / my school bag

2 José da Silva / our teacher

3 a visit to the zoo / a picnic in the country

4 writing English / speaking English

5 films / books

6 a flying boat / a plane

5 Complete the conversations with the correct preposition from the box.

> for in ~~on~~ on until with with

1 A: Did you go to Sam's party ....on...... Saturday evening?

B: Yes. I went .... Paulina.

2 A: I waited for you .... two o'clock! Where were you?

B: I was in my guitar lesson. I always have a guitar lesson .... Monday.

3 A: Were you at this school last year?

B: No, I wasn't. I came here .... September.

4 A: Where did you go on holiday last year?

B: I stayed .... my friend in Spain .... two weeks.

6 Read and complete the story. Use the past simple.

Bobby ¹ .... *lived* .... (live) in a flat in New York. Every day he ² .... (travel) to school by bus. He ³ .... (not walk) to school because the school ⁴ .... (be) a long way from his house. One day, Bobby ⁵ .... (want) to get to school before his friends. He ⁶ .... (start) to walk because it ⁷ .... (be) too early for the bus. He ⁸ .... (walk) and ⁹ .... (walk) for an hour. Where ¹⁰ .... (be) the school? He ¹¹ .... (ask) a man in a shop, 'Do you know where Main Street School is?' 'Yes,' the man ¹² .... (say). 'It's only five minutes from here.' When Bobby ¹³ .... (arrive) at school he ¹⁴ .... (be) very happy because he ¹⁵ .... (not be) late for class.

SPEAKING

7 Do an interview with an explorer.
Write questions with *be* in the past and present.
Ask and answer with your partner.

Where …
What kind of clothes/food …
How long/cold …
Why …
Who …

READING

8 A haiku is a short poem with three lines. Haikus are often about the weather. Read the haikus and match each one to a picture.

Snow
on the cold glass,
but inside it's warm.

Summer night –
in bed but not sleeping,
listening to the rain.

Long summer days,
there's no school for months.
Why am I sad?

The beach in winter,
cold wind in my face,
water in my shoes.

First snow of winter,
all the trees
have new clothes.

WRITING

9 Choose a picture and write your own haiku.

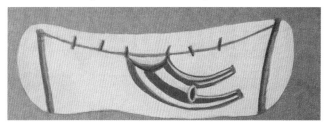

Activities

UNIT 4 Oh no! The chocolate! page 29 Exercise 8

UNIT 6 Have we got any eggs? page 41 Exercise 7

Conversation 1

Daniel:	Pedro, can you come to my swimming party?
Pedro:	Yes! When is it?
Daniel:	It's at 2.15, and it's at the swimming pool.
Pedro:	Great. Thanks!

Conversation 2

Hannah:	Would you like to come to my party, Melissa?
Melissa:	I'd love to! When is it?
Hannah:	It's on August 1st*.
Melissa:	What time?
Hannah:	From eight until late.
Melissa:	Cool!

Conversation 3

Andrew:	Sam, would you like to come to my football party?
Sam:	I'd love to. Is it at the park?
Andrew:	Yes, it is. It's on Saturday at 10 o'clock.
Sam:	I can't wait!

Conversation 4

Rebecca:	Can you come to my birthday party, Ella? It's on Wednesday, at my house.
Ella:	I'd love to, but what time is it?
Rebecca:	It's from 3.30 until 5.30.
Ella:	Oh, I'm sorry, I can't. I've got a guitar exam on Wednesday afternoon.

*August the first

UNIT 7 Eat a good breakfast! page 48

Answers: Good breakfasts are: 1, 3 and 4.

2 and 5 aren't good breakfasts. It isn't good for you to eat cake, sugar or chocolate for breakfast.

Activities

UNIT 13 Is there a cinema? page 81 Exercise 8

Look at the town plan. Label six buildings on the plan with place names.
Work in pairs. Ask and answer questions about your town plan.

A: Is there a restaurant in your town?
B: Yes, there is.
A: Where is it?
B: It's number four. It's a Turkish restaurant.

A: Hi, Suzie.

B: Hi, Danni. How are you doing?

A: Fine, thanks. And you?

B: I'm great!

A: Can you meet me this weekend?

B: I'd love to.

A: Let's go shopping. There's a sale on at the shopping centre.

B: Good idea! Shall we go on Saturday at 10 o'clock?

A: Yes, that's great. See you then.

B: And do you want to go swimming with me on Sunday morning?

A: Sorry, I can't.

Student A

Place E

The Blue Mosque

It's in Turkey.

It's about 400 years old.

Five million people visit it every year.

Place F

The Great Wall of China.

About 200 years old.

About 8 metres tall.

It is 7,200 kilometres long.

10 million people visit it every year.

The King:	My daughter, Natasha, isn't well. Please help me. Find something to make her better.
Ivan:	What can we do?
See-it-all:	We need the water of life. It's in another part of the world. I can see it. Here, Longlegs, take this cup and go and get the water of life.
Longlegs:	Here it is.
Ivan:	Here it is.
	Drink this. Please don't die.
Natasha:	Father, I don't want to die. I want Ivan to be my husband. He is a kind man and he has kind and clever friends. I love him very much.
The King:	Do you love my daughter?
Ivan:	Yes, I do.
The King:	Let's all live here together and be happy.

Activities

UNIT 17 José's house is newer page 103 Exercises 8 and 9

CULTURE: Important places around the world page 89 Exercise 7

Student B
Place G
The Great Sphinx
It's in Giza in Egypt.
It has the head of a human and
the body of a lion.
It is 4,500 years old.
About 5 million people visit it
every year.

Place H
The State Hermitage Museum
It's in Saint Petersburg, Russia.
It's a very big museum of Art.
It has over 3 million pictures.
It is about 250 years old.
The Winter Palace is part of the
Hermitage Museum. This was the home
of Russian emperors.
About 2.5 million people visit it every year.

REVIEW 2 UNITS 5–8 page 57 Exercise 8

COME TO MY PARTY!
DAY: ....
TIME: ....
PLACE: ....

Would you like to …?
It's on …
It's from … until …
It's at …
Can you bring some food?

When …?
What time …?
Where …?
Yes, I'd love to!
No, sorry, I can't.
Yes, I can bring some …

EP Vocabulary list

UNIT 1

Brazilian /brəˈzɪliən/ *noun*

camera /ˈkæmrə/ *noun*

Chinese /tʃaɪˈniːz/ *adjective*

dad /dæd/ *noun*

friend /frend/ *noun*

Greek /griːk/ *adjective*

Mexican /ˈmeksɪkən/ *adjective*

new /njuː/ *adjective*

phone /fəʊn/ *noun*

photo /ˈfəʊtəʊ/ *noun*

Russian /ˈrʌʃən/ *adjective*

teacher /ˈtiːtʃə/ *noun*

Turkish /ˈtɜːkɪʃ/ *adjective*

UNIT 2

bored /bɔːd/ *adjective*

brother /ˈbrʌðə/ *noun*

children /ˈtʃɪldrən/ *noun*

clever /ˈklevə/ *adjective*

dad /dæd/ *noun*

daughter /ˈdɔːtə/ *noun*

father /ˈfɑːðə/ *noun*

funny /ˈfʌni/ *adjective*

happy /ˈhæpi/ *adjective*

hot /hɒt/ *adjective*

hungry /ˈhʌŋgri/ *adjective*

husband /ˈhʌzbənd/ *noun*

mother /ˈmʌðə/ *noun*

mum /mʌm/ *noun*

nice /naɪs/ *adjective*

parents /ˈpeərənts/ *noun*

sad /sæd/ *adjective*

sister /ˈsɪstə/ *noun*

son /sʌn/ *noun*

tired /taɪəd/ *adjective*

wife /waɪf/ *noun*

UNIT 3

bath /bɑːθ/ *noun*

bathroom /'bɑːθrʊm/ *noun*

bed /bed/ *noun*

bedroom /'bedrʊm/ *noun*

chair /tʃeə/ *noun*

clock /klɒk/ *noun*

clothes /kləʊðz/ *noun*

computer /kəm'pjuːtə/ *noun*

computer game /kəm'pjuːtə ˌɡeɪm/ *noun*

DVD /diːviː'diː/ *noun*

floor /flɔː/ *noun*

guitar /ɡɪ'tɑː/ *noun*

kitchen /'kɪtʃən/ *noun*

living room /'lɪvɪŋ rʊm/ *noun*

pet /pet/ *noun*

shower /ʃaʊə/ *noun*

table /'teɪbl̩/ *noun*

toilet /'tɔɪlət/ *noun*

TV /tiː'viː/ *noun*

wall /wɔːl/ *noun*

window /'wɪndəʊ/ *noun*

UNIT 4

bag /bæɡ/ *noun*

ball /bɔːl/ *noun*

banana /bə'nɑːnə/ *noun*

big /bɪɡ/ *adjective*

chocolate /'tʃɒklət/ *noun*

clean /kliːn/ *adjective*

coat /kəʊt/ *noun*

dark /dɑːk/ *adjective*

dirty /'dɜːti/ *adjective*

drink /drɪŋk/ *noun*

football /'fʊtbɔːl/ *noun*

hat /hæt/ *noun*

key /kiː/ *noun*

light /laɪt/ *adjective*

long /lɒŋ/ *adjective*

old /əʊld/ *adjective*

short /ʃɔːt/ *adjective*

small /smɔːl/ *adjective*

EP Vocabulary list

UNIT 5

arm /ɑːm/ *noun*

ear /ɪə/ *noun*

eye /aɪ/ *noun*

face /feɪs/ *noun*

feet /fiːt/

foot /fʊt/ *noun*

hair /heə/ *noun*

hand /hænd/ *noun*

head /hed/ *noun*

leg /leg/ *noun*

mouth /maʊθ/ *noun*

nose /nəʊz/ *noun*

paint /peɪnt/ *verb*

play /pleɪ/ *verb*

ride /raɪd/ *verb*

sing /sɪŋ/ *verb*

speak /spiːk/ *verb*

swim /swɪm/ *verb*

teeth /tiːθ/ *noun*

tooth /tuːθ/ *noun*

UNIT 6

apple /ˈæpl̩/ *noun*

banana /bəˈnɑːnə/ *noun*

biscuit /ˈbɪskɪt/ *noun*

bread /bred/ *noun*

butter /ˈbʌtə/ *noun*

cheese /tʃiːz/ *noun*

egg /eg/ *noun*

flour /flaʊə/ *noun*

meat /miːt/ *noun*

milk /mɪlk/ *noun*

orange /ˈɒrɪndʒ/ *noun*

potato /pəˈteɪtəʊ/ *noun*

sugar /ˈʃʊgə/ *noun*

tomato /təˈmɑːtəʊ/ *noun*

UNIT 7

biscuit /ˈbɪskɪt/ *noun*

butter /ˈbʌtə/ *noun*

catch /kætʃ/ *verb*

chocolate /ˈtʃɒklət/ *noun*

dance /dɑːns/ *verb*

dancing /ˈdɑːntsɪŋ/ *noun*

kick /kɪk/ *verb*

orange /ˈɒrɪndʒ/ *noun*

play /pleɪ/ *verb*

run /rʌn/ *verb*

sugar /ˈʃʊgə/ *noun*

vegetable /ˈvedʒtəb‚l/ *noun*

walking /ˈwɔːkɪŋ/ *noun*

water /ˈwɔːtə/ *noun*

UNIT 8

club /klʌb/ *noun*

cooking /ˈkʊkɪŋ/ *noun*

do /duː/ *verb*

drawing /ˈdrɔːɪŋ/ *noun*

film /fɪlm/ *noun*

football /ˈfʊtbɔːl/ *noun*

guitar /gɪˈtɑː/ *noun*

horse riding /ˈhɔːs ˌraɪdɪŋ/ *noun*

make /meɪk/ *verb*

photo /ˈfəʊtəʊ/ *noun*

running /ˈrʌnɪŋ/ *noun*

tennis /ˈtenɪs/ *noun*

UNIT 9

catch /kætʃ/ *verb*

clean /kliːn/ *verb*

get dressed /get drest/

get up /get ʌp/ *phrase*

have /hæv/ *verb*

leave /liːv/ *verb*

wake up /weɪk ʌp/ *phrase*

walk /wɔːk/ *verb*

wash /wɒʃ/ *verb*

UNIT 10

art /ɑːt/ *noun*

download /daʊnˈləʊd/ *verb*

email /ˈiːmeɪl/ *noun*

English /ˈɪŋglɪʃ/ *noun*

geography /dʒiˈɒgrəfi/ *noun*

history /ˈhɪstəri/ *noun*

IT /aɪˈtiː/ *noun*

maths /mæθs/ *noun*

music /ˈmjuːzɪk/ *noun*

PE /ˌpiːˈiː/ *noun*

read /riːd/ *verb*

science /saɪəns/ *noun*

send /send/ *verb*

Spanish /ˈspænɪʃ/ *adjective*

store /stɔː/ *verb*

text /tekst/ *noun*

watch /wɒtʃ/ *verb*

website /ˈwebsaɪt/ *noun*

UNIT 11

band /bænd/ *noun*

come /kʌm/ *verb*

concert /ˈkɒnsət/ *noun*

famous /ˈfeɪməs/ *adjective*

fan /fæn/ *noun*

get /get/ *verb*

meet /miːt/ *verb*

movie /ˈmuːvi/ *noun*

newspaper /ˈnjuːzpeɪpə/ *noun*

see /siː/ *verb*

song /sɒŋ/ *noun*

things /θɪŋz/ *phrase*

think /θɪŋk *verb*

TV show /ˌtiːˈviː ʃəʊ/ *noun*

UNIT 12

chicken /ˈtʃɪkɪn/ *noun*

chips /tʃɪps/ *noun*

coffee /ˈkɒfi/ *noun*

doctor /ˈdɒktə/ *noun*

drive /draɪv/ *verb*

driver /ˈdraɪvə/ *noun*

fish /fɪʃ/ *noun*

ice cream /ˌaɪsˈkriːm/ *noun*

job /dʒɒb/ *noun*

learn /lɜːn/ *verb*

orange juice /ˈɒrɪndʒ dʒuːs/ *noun*

rice /raɪs/ *noun*

soup /suːp/ *noun*

student /ˈstjuːdənt/ *noun*

study /ˈstʌdi/ *verb*

teacher /ˈtiːtʃə/ *noun*

test /test/ *noun*

waitress /ˈweɪtrəs/ *noun*

work /wɜːk/ *verb, noun*

UNIT 13

bank /bæŋk/ *noun*

beautiful /ˈbjuːtɪfəl/ *adjective*

big /bɪg/ *adjective*

boring /ˈbɔːrɪŋ/ *adjective*

cheap /tʃiːp/ *adjective*

cinema /ˈsɪnəmə/ *noun*

exciting /ɪkˈsaɪtɪŋ/ *adjective*

expensive /ɪkˈspensɪv/ *adjective*

great /greɪt/ *adjective*

hospital /ˈhɒspɪtəl/ *noun*

hotel /həʊˈtel/ *noun*

important /ɪmˈpɔːtənt/ *adjective*

interesting /ˈɪntrəstɪŋ/ *adjective*

little /ˈlɪtl̩/ *adjective*

museum /mjuːˈziːəm/ *noun*

new /njuː/ *adjective*

old /əʊld/ *adjective*

restaurant /ˈrestrɒnt/ *noun*

safe /seɪf/ *adjective*

short /ʃɔːt/ *adjective*

station /ˈsteɪʃən/ *noun*

tall /tɔːl/ *adjective*

university /ˌjuːnɪˈvɜːsɪti/ *noun*

UNIT 14

cow /kaʊ/ *noun*

grass /grɑːs/ *noun*

picnic /ˈpɪknɪk/ *noun*

river /ˈrɪvə/ *noun*

tree /triː/ *noun*

UNIT 15

beard /bɪəd/ *noun*

beautiful /ˈbjuːtɪfəl/ *adjective*

dark /dɑːk/ *adjective*

dress /dres/ *noun*

fat /fæt/ *adjective*

glasses /ˈglɑːsɪz/ *noun*

hat /hæt/ *noun*

jacket /ˈdʒækɪt/ *noun*

jeans /dʒiːnz/ *noun*

long /lɒŋ/ *adjective*

old /əʊld/ *adjective*

shirt /ʃɜːt/ *noun*

shoe /ʃuː/ *noun*

short /ʃɔːt/ *adjective*

skirt /skɜːt/ *noun*

slim /slɪm/ *adjective*

tall /tɔːl/ *adjective*

trousers /ˈtraʊzəz/ *noun*

T-shirt /ˈtiːʃɜːt/ *noun*

watch /wɒtʃ/ *noun*

young /jʌŋ/ *adjective*

UNIT 16

clothes /kləʊðz/ *noun*

cup /kʌp/ *noun*

dollar /ˈdɒlə/ *noun*

euro /ˈjʊərəʊ/ *noun*

flower /ˈflaʊə/ *noun*

paint /peɪnt/ *noun*

pence /pents/ *noun*

plate /pleɪt/ *noun*

pound /paʊnd/ *noun*

toy /tɔɪ/ *noun*

UNIT 17

beach /biːtʃ/ *noun*

cat /kæt/ *noun*

garden /ˈgɑːdən/ *noun*

house /haʊs/ *noun*

rainforest /ˈreɪnfɒrɪst/ *noun*

ride /raɪd/ *noun*

safari /səˈfɑːri/ *noun*

sea /siː/ *noun*

story /ˈstɔːri/ *noun*

EP Vocabulary list

UNIT 18

beach /biːtʃ/ *noun*

cold /kəʊld/ *adjective*

cow /kaʊ/ *noun*

cup /kʌp/ *noun*

dog /dɒg/ *noun*

family /ˈfæməli/ *noun*

farm /fɑːm/ *noun*

hot /hɒt/ *adjective*

plate /pleɪt/ *noun*

rain /reɪn/ *noun*

sea /siː/ *noun*

sheep /ʃiːp/ *noun*

snow /snəʊ/ *noun*

summer /ˈsʌmə/ *noun*

sun /sʌn/ *noun*

tent /tent/ *noun*

warm /wɔːm/ *adjective*

weather /ˈweðə/ *noun*

wind /wɪnd/ *noun*

winter /ˈwɪntə/ *noun*

UNIT 19

band /bænd/ *noun*

bus /bʌs/ *noun*

car /kɑː/ *noun*

late /leɪt/ *adjective*

ticket /ˈtɪkɪt/ *noun*

end /end/ *noun*

hat /hæt/ *noun*

knife /naɪf/ *noun*

late /leɪt/ *adjective*

money /ˈmʌni/ *noun*

notebook /ˈnəʊtbʊk/ *noun*

plane /pleɪn/ *noun*

tent /tent/ *noun*

ticket /ˈtɪkɪt/ *noun*

tired /taɪəd/ *adjective*

trousers /ˈtraʊzəz/ *noun*

T-shirt /ˈtiːʃɜːt/ *noun*

water bottle /ˈwɔːtə ˈbɒtˌl/ *noun*

UNIT 20

bird /bɜːd/ *noun*

boat /bəʊt/ *noun*

flying /ˈflaɪ.ɪŋ/ *adjective*

poor /pɔː/ *adjective*

poster /ˈpəʊstə/ *noun*

tree /triː/ *noun*

Grammar reference

UNIT 1
DETERMINERS

I	my	*My name is Oliver.*
you	your	*This is your phone.*
he	his	*This is his camera.*
she	her	*Her name isn't Rosa.*

Practice

1 Complete the sentences.

0 This is Michael. He's ...my... brother.

1 What's .... phone number? My number's 076 355 243.

2 This is my brother, ... name's David.

3 Hi, I'm Sam. What's............ name?

4 This is Jenny. She's .... sister.

5 This is my friend, ... name's Sarah.

6 Oh no! Where's .... phone?

2 Circle the correct word.

0 My mum's from America. (Her)/ His name's Martha.

1 *My / His* name's Samantha.

2 Hi, my name's Joe. What's *your / my* name?

3 Is this your camera? No, *my / her* camera's white.

4 This isn't Tom's phone. *Your / His* phone's blue!

5 Is this my book? Yes, *her / your* name is on it.

6 Hello. This is my sister and this is *her / his* friend, Jack.

7 My English teacher's new. *His / Her* name's Janet Smithers.

8 This is a photo of my dad. *Your / His* name's Jim.

BE

Positive (+)	
I **am** = I'**m**	*I'm from Australia.*
You **are** = You'**re**	*You're English.*
He **is** = He'**s**	*He's my brother.*
She **is** = She'**s**	*She's my sister.*
It **is** = It'**s**	*It's my camera.*
We **are** = We'**re**	*We're from Brazil.*
They **are** = They'**re**	*They're Greek.*
Negative (–)	
I **am not** = I'**m not**	*I'm not Italian.*
You **are not** = You **aren't**	*You aren't French.*
He **is not** = He **isn't**	*He isn't my teacher.*
She **is not** = She **isn't**	*She isn't Spanish.*
It **is not** = It **isn't**	*It isn't your book.*
We **are not** = We **aren't**	*We aren't French.*
They **are not** = They **aren't**	*They aren't English.*

Practice

3 Complete the sentences with a pronoun and the positive or negative form of *be*.

0 This is Tom. ..He's.. my friend.

1 Happy Birthday! .... twelve today!

2 This is Diana. .... my friend.

3 I'm Stefanos and this is Daska. We're Greek, ... Spanish.

4 This is Michael. .... my brother, he's my friend.

5 Hello, My name's Mr Green. .... your new English teacher.

6 Look at my new camera. .... so cool!

7 My camera's old. .... very good.

8 This is Paola from Rome. .... Italian.

9 Your name's Yuki. .... from Japan, is that right?

10 Sorry, ... in this class. You're in room 5.

4 Complete the conversation.

Tom: Hi. **(1)** .... Tom.

Nora: Hello, **(2)** .... name's Nora.

Tom: This **(3)** .... Ben. **(4)** .... my friend. It's **(5)** .... birthday today. **(6)** .... twelve.

Nora: Happy birthday, Ben! Today's my birthday and **(7)** .... twelve too! And this is **(8)** .... new camera.

Tom and Ben: Happy Birthday!

Tom: Your camera **(9)** .... cool!

UNIT 2

DETERMINERS: *OUR* AND *THEIR*

we	our	*Our mum is funny.*
they	their	*Is that their dog?*

Practice

1 Complete the sentences with *my, your, his, her, its, our, their*.

0 This is George and Sarah, they are ...my... mum's friends.

1 Alessandro and Laura live in England, but .... dad's from Argentina.

2 Hi! We're James and Charlotte and this is .... dog, Spotty.

3 Is that your brother? What's .... name?

4 Hi Dan, is .... sister at school?

5 This is Anna. It's .... birthday today!

6 Is that your school? What's .... name?

POSSESSIVE *'S*

This is my mum's cat. It is her cat. **Not** ~~This is the cat of my mum.~~

This is Jake and Nat's dog. It is their dog. **Not** ~~This is the dog of Jake and Nat.~~

2 Look at the picture and complete the sentences with the correct names and 's.

1 Sally is ...., ... and .... mother.

2 Nat is .... and .... son and .... and .... brother.

3 Jason is ...., ... and .... father.

4 Katie is .... and .... sister and .... and .... daughter.

5 Sally is .... wife.

6 Jason is .... husband.

BE

Questions (?)	Short answers (+)	Short answers (−)
Am I funny?	Yes, you **are**.	No, you **aren't**.
Are you English?	Yes, I **am**.	No, I'm **not**.
Is he tired?	Yes, he **is**.	No, he **isn't**.
Is she Spanish?	Yes, she **is**.	No, she **isn't**.
Is it hot?	Yes, it **is**.	No, it **isn't**.
Are we happy?	Yes, we **are**.	No, we **aren't**.
Are they your parents?	Yes they **are**.	No, they **aren't**.

How old **is he**? **not** ~~How old he is?~~
Where **are you** from? **not** ~~Where you are from?~~

3 Read the sentences and write *plural*, *is*, or *possessive*.

0 Peter's brother is called Frank ___possessive___

1 I have two sisters. ....

2 My brother's phone is red. ....

3 My favourite films are cartoons. ....

4 Sara's from Finland. ....

5 Peter is Luke's son. ....

6 Jack's English. ....

7 My books are here. ....

4 Write the sentences as questions.

0 Peter is American.
   ...Is Peter American?...........

1 They are from Italy.
   ....

2 You are happy.
   ....

3 We are late.
   ....

4 She is hungry.
   ....

5 They are Italian.
   ....

6 Mary is from Ireland.
   ....

7 They are sad.
   ....

5 Complete the short answers for the questions in Exercise 4.

0 Yes, _he is._   4 Yes, ...
1 No, ...   5 No, ...
2 Yes, ...   6 Yes, ...
3 No, ...   7 No, ...

UNIT 3

THERE IS / THERE ARE

there's (there is)
There's a TV in the living room.
There's a picture on the wall.
There's a shower in the bathroom.
there are
There are two tables in the kitchen.
There are three people in the kitchen.
There are two beds in the bedroom.

Practice

1 Look at the picture and complete the sentences with *there's* and *there are*.

0 ....There's........... a bed.
1 .... a shower.
2 .... four chairs
3 .... a table.
4 .... a lot of windows.
5 .... a boy in the kitchen.

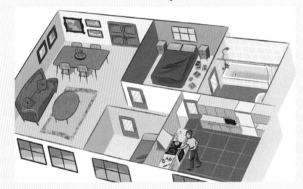

IN/ON

*Mum is **in** the bathroom.*
*There's a dictionary **on** my desk.*

*I live **in** a house.*
*The camera is **on** the floor.*

Practice

2 Complete the sentences with *in* or *on*.

0 There's a guitar ....on.... the bed.
1 I've got a computer .... my bedroom.
2 There are two pictures .... the wall.
3 There are some books .... the table.
4 There's a shower and a bath .... the bathroom.
5 All my computer games are .... the floor.
6 There are four chairs and a table .... the kitchen.

HAVE GOT

I**'ve got** (have got)	*I**'ve got** a phone.*
You**'ve got** (have got)	*You**'ve got** a guitar.*
He**'s got** (has got)	*He**'s got** two pet fish.*
She**'s got** (has got)	*She**'s got** a nice flat.*
It**'s got** (has got)	*It**'s got** a big living room.*
We**'ve got** (have got)	*We**'ve got** lots of DVDs.*
They**'ve got** (have got)	*They**'ve got** a TV in their bedroom.*

Practice

3 Look at the table and complete the sentences with *have / has got*.

	Me	My dad	Rosa and David
camera	0 ✔	✗	5 ✔
dictionary	✗	2 ✔	✗
mobile phone	✗	3 ✔	6 ✔
guitar	1 ✔	✗	✗
radio	✗	4 ✔	✗

0 I've got a camera.
1 ....
2 ....
3 ....
4 He ....
5 ....
6 They ....

UNIT 4

HAVE GOT ⊖, *HAVE GOT* ❓

have got (–)	*have got (?)*	Short answers
I **haven't got**	**Have** I **got**?	Yes, you **have**. No, you **haven't**.
You **haven't got**	**Have** you **got**?	Yes, I **have**. No, I **haven't**.
He **hasn't got**	**Has** he **got**?	Yes, he **has**. No, he **hasn't**.
She **hasn't got**	**Has** she **got**?	Yes, she **has**. No, she **hasn't**.
It **hasn't got**	**Has** it **got**?	Yes, it **has**. No, it **hasn't**.
We **haven't got**	**Have** we **got**?	Yes, we **have**. No, we **haven't**.
They **haven't got**	**Have** they **got**?	Yes, they **have**. No, they **haven't**.

*I **haven't got** a bike.   He **hasn't got** a dog.*
*We **haven't got** any chocolate.*
***Has** she **got** a new phone? Yes, she **has**.*

Practice

1 **Complete the sentences with *haven't / hasn't got*.**

   0 Tony .hasn't.got. a pet fish.
   1 We .... a shower in our bathroom.
   2 The teacher isn't happy! Jane .... her book.
   3 Andy's cold. He .... a hat and coat.
   4 Jackie's hungry. She .... an apple or a banana.
   5 Jim and Ellen .... their guitars.
   6 My mum and dad .... new mobile phones.

2 **Look at the table and write sentences about Emma, Tom and Ben.**

	Emma	Tom and Ben	(you) put ✔ or ✘
a phone	✔	✘	....
the keys	✔	✘	....
a notebook	✘	✔	....
a pet fish	✘	✔	....
a hat	✔	✘	....

   0 Emma / a phone / a notebook:
   Emma's got a phone but she hasn't got a notebook.
   1 Tom and Ben: a notebook / a phone

   ....
   2 Emma: a hat / a pet fish

   ....
   3 Tom and Ben: the keys / a pet fish

   ....
   4 Emma: the keys

   ....

3 **Now complete the table about you. Write ✔ or ✘. Then write the complete sentences.**

   1 I / a phone / a pet fish: ....
   ....
   2 I / a hat / the keys ....
   ....
   3 I / notebook ....
   ....

4 **Match the questions with the answers.**

   0 [a] Has Sally got a pet?
   1 [ ] Have you got a drink?
   2 [ ] Has Jane got her notebook?
   3 [ ] Has Andrew got a phone?
   4 [ ] Have we got the chocolate?
   5 [ ] Have I got your telephone number?
   6 [ ] Have you got your keys?

   a Yes, she has. She's got a dog.
   b No, she hasn't. It's at home.
   c Yes, we have. Here it is!
   d No, you haven't. It's 939 405 372.
   e Yes, he has. It's in his school bag.
   f Yes, I have. They're in my coat.
   g No, I haven't. Is there a cola?

5 **Write questions with *have / has got*.**

   0 Rebecca / a new car?
   Has Rebecca got a new car?
   1 Holly / a dark blue phone?

   ....
   2 Mary and Paolo / a new computer?

   ....
   3 You / your glasses?

   ....
   4 William and Susie / their hats and coats?

   ....
   5 Your brother / a red camera?

   ....
   6 Your sister / a ruler in her pencil case?

   ....

UNIT 5

CAN / CAN'T

Positive (+)	Negative (−)
I **can dance**.	I **can't sing**.
You **can dance**.	You **can't sing**.
He **can dance**.	He **can't sing**.
She **can dance**.	She **can't sing**.
It **can dance**.	It **can't sing**.
We **can dance**.	We **can't sing**.
They **can dance**.	They **can't sing**.
Questions (?)	**Short answers**
Can I **talk**?	Yes, you **can**. No, you **can't**.
Can you **talk**?	Yes, I **can**. No, I **can't**.
Can he **talk**?	Yes, he **can**. No, he **can't**.
Can she **talk**?	Yes, she **can**. No, she **can't**.
Can it **talk**?	Yes, it **can**. No, it **can't**.
Can we **talk**?	Yes, we **can**. No, we **can't**.
Can they **talk**?	Yes, they **can**. No, they **can't**.

Practice

1 Complete the sentences with *can* or *can't*.

0 I .*can't*. swim.

1 Mary .... speak Russian very well. ✔

2 Thomas .... take very good photos with his phone. ✘

3 We .... play the guitar. ✘

4 Jane and Roberta .... paint pictures very well. ✔

5 My mother .... sing. ✘

6 I .... ride a horse. ✔

2 Write the questions and short answers.

0 he / play the piano?   No, ...
   ....*Can he play the piano?*....   No, he can't.

1 they / paint pictures?   Yes, ...

2 you / ride a horse?   No, ...

3 your sister / take good photos?   Yes, ...

4 Lizzy and Rita / swim underwater? No, ...

5 you and Martha / play the guitar? Yes, ...

6 Martin / speak Chinese?   No, ...

3 Look at the table and answer the questions.

Sally	Tom	Jack	Meg	Pier
Meg	Pier	Sally	Philippe	Tom
Pier	Jack	Philippe	Tom	Sally

0 Who can sing?
   Pier, Tom and Sally can sing.

1 Who can speak Italian?
....

2 Who can't swim underwater?
....

3 Who can paint and ride a horse?
....

4 Who can't sing but can speak Italian?
....

5 Who can ride a horse but can't sing?
....

4 Write 4 sentences about what you can and can't do.

0 *I can paint but I can't swim* *underwater.*

1 ....

2 ....

3 ....

4 ....

PREPOSITIONS: *INTO, BEHIND, UNDER*

*Let's go **into** the classroom now.*
*Where's Dan? I can't see him. He's **behind** the wall.*
*Your pencil is **under** the book.*

Practice

5 Write the correct preposition: *into, under* or *behind*.

1 Go .... the classroom, please.

2 Put your bag .... the door.

3 Put your coat .... your bag.

4 The cat's .... the desk.

5 Get .... bed now!

6 Look! Tom's .... the cupboard!

UNIT 6

SOME, ANY, LOTS OF

	Countable nouns	Uncountable nouns
Some		
Positive sentences	We made **some** cakes.	There is **some** milk in the fridge.
Offers	Would you like **some** apples?	Would you like **some** water?
Any		
Negative sentences	We didn't make **any** cakes.	There isn't **any** milk in the fridge.
Questions	Are there **any** cakes?	Is there **any** milk in the fridge?
Lots of		
Positive sentences	We've got **lots of** cakes.	There's **lots of** sugar.

Practice

1 Complete the sentences with *any* or *some*.

1 Is there .... butter?
2 We've got .... milk.
3 Are there .... tomatoes?
4 Would you like .... chocolate?
5 Has Mary got .... eggs?
6 There aren't .... people here.

2 Look at the recipe and then complete the dialogue with *some, any* or *lots of*.

> ### RECIPE
> For this fantastic 'Chocbanana' cake you need:
>
> - eggs
> - sugar
> - milk
> - flour
> - butter
> - chocolate

In the fridge they've got:

Mum: Let's make a birthday cake, Katie! Look in the fridge!

Katie: OK, Mum, we've got **(1)** .... milk and **(2)** .... bananas.

Mum: Have we got **(3)** .... butter?

Katie: No, we haven't. And we haven't got **(4)** .... eggs.

Mum: What? No, look, Katie, there are **(5)** .... eggs here! There are 12!

Katie: Oh yes, good! Have we got **(6)** .... flour?

Mum: No, we haven't. It's on the shopping list.

Katie: The recipe says chocolate, is there **(7)** .... chocolate?

Mum: Oh no, there isn't. Let's go to the supermarket and buy **(8)** ....!

PREPOSITIONS: *ON, AT, FROM, UNTIL*

on + days and dates	**on** Monday, **on** Saturday, **on** 12th March
at + places	**at** my house, **at** the park, **at** the cinema
from ... until + times	**from** 9 am **until** 3 pm

Practice

3 Complete the dialogue with *at, on, from ... until*.

Dave: Would you like to come to my party?

Jenny: I'd love to. When is it?

Dave: It's **(1)** .... 18th July, that's next week.

Jenny: Where is it?

Dave: It's **(2)** .... my house.

Jenny: What time is the party?

Dave: It's **(3)** .... 8 pm **(4)** .... 11 pm.

Jenny: Great! See you **(5)** .... Thursday then.

UNIT 7

LIKE

Positive (+)	Negative (–)
I **like** dancing.	I **don't like** running.
You **like** dancing.	You **don't like** running.
He **likes** dancing.	He **doesn't like** running.
She **likes** dancing.	She **doesn't like** running.
We **like** dancing.	We **don't like** running.
They **like** dancing.	They **don't like** running.

Practice

1 Complete the sentences with *like / likes, don't like / doesn't like.*

1 I .... playing basketball. ☺

2 Jo .... dancing. ☺

3 We .... chocolate. ☹

4 You .... football. ☹

5 Dan and Megan .... swimming. ☺

6 He .... computer games. ☹

2 Complete the sentences with *like / likes, don't like / doesn't like* so they are true for you and your family.

0 I *don't like* doing homework.

1 My mum .... cooking.

2 My dad .... driving.

3 My brother and sister .... swimming.

4 I .... playing tennis.

5 I .... riding horses.

6 My parents .... going to the cinema.

PRONOUNS

I	me	Do you like **me**?
you	you	Bananas are good for **you**.
he	him	I don't like **him**.
she	her	This present is for **her**.
it	it	We don't like tennis. We aren't good at **it**.
we	us	Can you help **us**?
they	them	They're very nice. I like **them**.

Practice

3 Circle the correct pronoun.

0 Kate is very kind. I like (her)/ she a lot.

1 I like playing tennis. It's good for *I / me*.

2 Mina eats lots of vegetables. She likes *them / they* a lot.

3 Do you like *we / us*?

4 Paul doesn't like playing computer games all day. It isn't good for *him / he*.

5 Jake and Tina are very nice. I like *they / them*.

6 My sister likes running. I run with *she / her* sometimes.

UNIT 8

PRESENT CONTINUOUS

Positive (+)	Negative (−)
I'm (am) cooking.	I'm not (am not) reading.
You're (are) cooking.	You aren't (are not) reading.
He's (is) cooking.	He isn't (is not) reading.
She's (is) cooking.	She isn't (is not) reading.
It's (is) cooking.	It isn't (is not) reading.
We're (are) cooking.	We aren't (are not) reading.
They're (are) cooking.	They aren't (are not) reading.
Questions (?)	Short answers
Am I sleeping?	Yes, you are. No, you aren't.
Are you sleeping?	Yes, I am. No, I'm not.
Is he sleeping?	Yes, he is. No, he isn't.
Is she sleeping?	Yes, she is. No, she isn't.
Is it sleeping?	Yes, it is. No, it isn't.
Are we sleeping?	Yes, we are. No, we aren't.
Are they sleeping?	Yes, they are. No, they aren't.

Spelling

read + -ing	Sam's reading a book.
swim + -m + -ing	Sarah's swimming in the pool.
dance + -ing	We're dancing to the music.

Practice

1 Write the *-ing* form of the verbs.

1 swim ....   5 kick ....   9 sit ....
2 write ....   6 ride ....   10 clean ....
3 come ....   7 look ....
4 wash ....   8 know ....

2 Look at the picture and complete the sentences with a verb from the list.

> talk   play   dance   sing   take   paint

0 Freddy*'s taking* photos.
1 Chris .... the guitar.
2 Susie and Jane ....
3 Carla .... on her phone.
4 Ben and Paul .... a picture.
5 Sally ....

3 Write the sentences in Exercise 2 in the negative form.

0 *Freddy isn't taking photos.*
1 ....
2 ....
3 ....
4 ....
5 ....

4 Look at the picture in Exercise 2 and complete the questions and short answers.

0 ...Is... Chris ...playing the guitar... ?
Yes, ...he is.. .
1 Is Freddy dancing?
....
2 .... Susie and Jane .... ?
....
3 .... Carla painting?
....
4 .... Ben .... ?
Yes, ...
5 .... Chris and Sally .... ?
Yes, ...

UNIT 9

PRESENT SIMPLE

Positive (+)	Negative (−)
I **work**.	I **don't work**.
You **work**.	You **don't work**.
He **works**.	He **doesn't work**.
She **works**.	She **doesn't work**.
It **works**.	It **doesn't work**.
We **work**.	We **don't work**.
They **work**.	They **don't work**.

*They **work** all day.*
*She **gets** the bus to school.*
*They **don't play** basketball on Tuesdays.*
*He **doesn't go** cycling at the weekend.*

Practice

1 **Complete the sentences with the correct form of the present simple of the verbs in brackets.**

0 I .start. (start) school at 9 o'clock.

1 Jack .... (wake up) at 6.30 am.

2 We .... (clean) our teeth in the morning and the evening.

3 They .... (get up) at 7 o'clock.

4 I .... (wash) my face in the morning.

5 Fiona .... (have) a big breakfast.

6 You .... (catch) the bus at 8 o'clock.

7 He .... (finish) school at 3.30 pm.

2 **Write the sentences in Exercise 1 in the negative form.**

0 *I don't start school at 9 o'clock.* ....

1 ....

2 ....

3 ....

4 ....

5 ....

6 ....

7 ....

3 **Write sentences.**

0 Laura / get up / 08.00   *Laura gets up at eight o'clock.* ....

1 I / breakfast / room / then / dressed   ....

2 They / not catch bus / walk / school   ....

3 Harry / not walk / school / go / dad's car   ....

4 Tony / breakfast / bedroom / not / kitchen   ....

5 You / go / school / 07.30 / you / not / go school / 08.30

UNIT 10

PRESENT SIMPLE: QUESTIONS AND SHORT ANSWERS

Questions (?)	Short answers
Do I **walk** to school?	Yes, you **do**. No, you **don't**.
Do you **use** IT in English lessons?	Yes, I **do**. No, I **don't**.
Does he **like** cooking?	Yes, he **does**. No, he **doesn't**.
Does she **go** to school on Saturdays?	Yes, she **does**. No, she **doesn't**.
Does it **work**?	Yes, it **does**. No, it **doesn't**.
Do we **have** History on Wednesdays?	Yes, we **do**. No, we **don't**.
Do they **speak** French?	Yes, they **do**. No, they **don't**.

Practice

1 Write the questions.

0 Martin / like / maths
   Does Martin like maths?

1 your friends / go /school / car
   .... ?

2 Mr Harvey / teach / English
   .... ?

3 Tony / play / computer games / evening
   .... ?

4 you / have / P.E. / Monday
   .... ?

5 Maria's dad / watch / a lot / TV
   .... ?

2 Write the short answers.

0 Does Susy like Art?   (✔)
1 Do you get up at eight o'clock?   (✘)
2 Do Mark and Tony walk to school?   (✔)
3 Does Maria study Science at school? (✘)
4 Do the students have P.E. on Friday? (✘)
5 Does your dad like geography?   (✔)
   Yes, she does.
   ....
   ....
   ....
   ....
   ....

HOW MUCH ...? / HOW MANY ...?

Countable nouns	Uncountable nouns
How many ...?	How much ...?
How many texts do you send a week?	How much fruit do you eat a day?

How many people are there in the classroom?
There are 25.
How much money have you got?
I've got £5.

Practice

3 Complete the question with *How much* or *How many* and a verb from the list.

> take   send   watch   store
> look at   get   send   download

0 .How. .much. homework do you ...get... in a day?

1 .... texts do you .... in a day?

2 .... television do you .... in a day?

3 .... music do you .... in a week?

4 .... emails do you........... in a week?

5 .... information do you .... in a week?

6 .... websites do you .... in a day?

7 .... photos do you .... in a week?

4 Answer the questions in Exercise 3 so they are true for you.

0 I get lots of homework.
1 ....
2 ....
3 ....
4 ....
5 ....
6 ....
7 ....

UNIT 11

ADVERBS OF FREQUENCY: *ALWAYS, OFTEN, SOMETIMES, NEVER*

always   often   sometimes   never

always, often, sometimes and ***never*** go:
* before most verbs.
  You ***always take*** your phone to school.
  Jane ***sometimes does*** her homework in bed.
* after the verb ***be***.
  We ***are never*** late for school.
  I ***am often*** sad on Sunday evenings.

Practice

1 Write the sentences with the adverb in the correct place.

0 Jack goes to the theatre. (never)
  Jack never goes to the theatre.

1 Katia is late for school. (never)

2 We go to the cinema on Monday evenings. (always)

3 I play tennis with my friends at the weekends. (sometimes)

4 They are at school from Monday to Friday. (always)

5 Joe likes making cakes. (often)

6 I take photos on holiday. (often)

2 How often do you do these things? Write sentences.

Frequency	Part A	Part B	when
♀♀♀♀	do	my homework	in the morning
♀♀♀♀	go	on the internet	in the evening
♀♀♀♀	play	tennis	on Thursday
♀♀♀♀	watch	TV	in the afternoon
♀♀♀♀	listen	to music	at the weekend
♀♀♀♀	ride	my horse	on Sunday

0 *I never do my homework in the morning.*
1
2
3
4
5

WH- QUESTIONS

Who?	a person	Rachel, my sister
Where?	a place	New York, England, the cinema, school
When?	a time / day	Sunday, 5 o'clock, now
What?	a thing	tennis, a bag, films
How often?	every day, week	every Tuesday, sometimes

Practice

3 Write the question word *who*, *where*, *when*, *what* or *how often*.

1 .... ?
  A party!
2 .... ?
  At my house.
3 .... ?
  On January 10th.
4 .... ?
  Maria, Jack, Silvia, Ben, Marta and Tony
5 .... ?
  Every year!

UNIT 12

PRESENT SIMPLE AND PRESENT CONTINUOUS

→ For present continuous see Unit 8, page 144.
→ For present simple see Units 9 & 10, pages 145–146.

We use the **present simple** to talk about:
- what we do every day.
  I go to school.   My dad drives a taxi.
- What we always / sometimes / never do.
  You always get up late on Sundays.
  Katie sometimes has dinner at 6 o'clock.

We use the **present continuous** to talk about what we are doing now:
Jess is sleeping.   We're studying English.

Practice

1 Circle the correct verb.

1 It's half past nine, Tommy's at school and *he studies / he's studying*.

2 Every day Jacob *gets up / is getting up* at seven o'clock.

3 My mum's in the bathroom, she *has / is having* a shower.

4 Our history teacher always *gives / is giving* us a lot of homework.

5 I often *play / am playing* volleyball in the park on Sunday.

6 Mrs Weston *likes / is liking* her job. She's a police officer.

7 The children are in class seven at the moment. They *do / are doing* a geography test.

8 Marta *doesn't speak / isn't speaking* German very well – she never studies!

2 Write questions in the present simple or continuous using *what / doing?* or *what / do?*

0 *What does Marco do?*
  Marco? He works in a bank in London.

1 .... ?
  I can't speak! I'm in the cinema!

2 .... ?
  Every Sunday? She goes to church.

3 .... ?
  I'm a teacher. I teach Spanish.

4 .... ?
  I'm hungry! This is my lunch.

5 .... ?
  Carla? She's in the shower.

6 .... ?
  Phillip's a dentist and Julie is a nurse.

7 .... ?
  Ben? His homework, he's in his room.

CAN: REQUESTS AND PERMISSION

Requests	Can I have some milk, please?
	Can you open the window, please?
Permission	Can I go out with my friends, Mum?

Practice

3 Write *Can I* or *Can you,* then finish the requests with words from the box.

> the dishes, please   some soup, please
> the table   me with my homework
> a film, please   me in the park
> your camera, please   home, please

0 Can ..*you*.. wash ..*the dishes please*.. ?
  ..*request*..

1 Can .... go .... ?
  ....

2 Can .... clean .... ?
  ....

3 Can .... meet .... ?
  ....

4 Can .... watch .... ?
  ....

5 Can .... have .... ?
  ....

6 Can .... use .... ?
  ....

7 Can .... help .... ?
  ....

4 Write *request* or *permission* next to 1–7 in Exercise 3.

UNIT 13

IS THERE A ...? / ARE THERE ANY ...?

Questions (?)	Short answers
Is there a bank here?	Yes, **there is**. No, **there isn't**.
Are there any people outside?	Yes, **there are**. No, **there aren't**.

Practice

1 **Circle the correct words.**

0 (*Is*) / *Are* there a supermarket near here?

1 There *isn't* / *aren't* any museums in my town.

2 *Is* / *Are* there any good museums near here?

3 *Is* / *Are* there a bank on this street?

4 *There isn't* / *aren't* a hospital here.

5 *There 's* / *are* a great restaurant we can eat in.

6 *There 's* / *are* lots of students in my school.

2 **Complete the questions about a town with *Is there a?* or *Are there any?* and complete the short answers.**

0 ...Is there a... museum?   ...Yes, there is...

1 .... banks?   Yes, ...

2 .... schools?   Yes, ...

3 .... cafés?   No, ...

4 .... hospital?   Yes, ...

5 .... station?   No, ...

6 .... cinemas?   Yes, ...

7 .... university?   No, ...

8 .... hotels?   Yes, ...

9 .... supermarkets?   Yes, ...

PREPOSITIONS: *INSIDE, OUTSIDE, ABOVE, BELOW, NEAR*

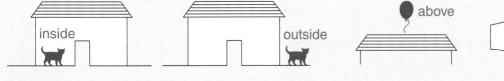 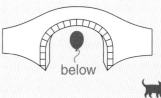

Practice

3 **Where's the ball? Use the words in the box.**

> inside   near   outside   above   below

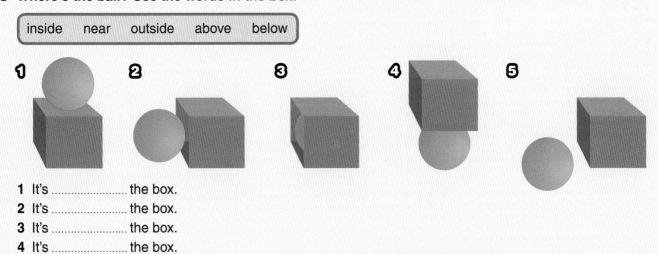

1 It's .... the box.

2 It's .... the box.

3 It's .... the box.

4 It's .... the box.

5 It's .... the box.

UNIT 14

WHY ...? BECAUSE

Why ...?	Because ...
Why are you running?	**Because** I'm late.
Why do you eat fruit?	**Because** I like it.

Practice

1 Put the words in order to make questions.

0 John / why / eating / is / big / that / sandwich?

..Why is John eating that big sandwich?..

1 birds / go / why / do / south / winter / in?

....

2 you / looking / the / under / table / why / are?

....

3 aren't / coming / to / they / party / our / why?

....

4 Nat / Katie / river / running / why / are / and / the / to?

....

5 a / want / do / doctor / be / to / why / you?

....

6 Peter / walk / why / school / to / does / day / every?

....

7 Buying / why / you / that / camera / new / are?

....

2 Match the questions in Exercise 1 to the answers a–h below.

a Because he's hungry. [0]

b Because I can't find mine. ☐

c Because I want to help people. ☐

d Because the dog is there. ☐

e Because they're looking for warm temperatures. ☐

f Because they're on holiday. ☐

g Because they're going swimming. ☐

h Because it's good for him. ☐

LET'S ..., SHALL WE ...?

Let's	**Let's** have a party. **Let's** have a pizza for dinner.	I'd love to. Yes, that's a great idea. Sorry, I can't.
Shall we	**Shall we** go to the beach this weekend**?** **Shall we** watch a DVD later**?**	

Practice

3 Complete the sentences with *Shall we?* or *Let's* and a verb from the box.

meet   watch   go x2
play   do   visit

0 ..Shall we go.. to the cinema?

1 .... football in the park.

2 .... shopping at the weekend?

3 .... our grandparents this weekend?

4 .... outside the Science Museum.

5 .... a DVD.

6 .... our homework.

4 Match suggestions 1–6 in Exercise 3 with the replies.

a Yes, that's a good idea. There's an interesting film at the Odeon. [0]

b Sorry we can't. Our DVD player doesn't work. ☐

c That's a good idea. Let's do maths first. ☐

d Oh yes, I'd love to! Can I be on your team? ☐

e Oh yes, I'd love to. I like going to their house. ☐

f That's a great idea. See you there at 10 o'clock, OK? ☐

g Sorry, I can't. I haven't got any money. ☐

UNIT 15

PLURALS – SPELLING

always plural	clothes, jeans, glasses, trousers
add -s	house → houses, skirt → skirts, cinema → cinemas
add -es	bus → buses, box → boxes, sandwich → sandwiches
change -y to -ies	baby → babies, dictionary → dictionaries

Practice

1 **Write the words in the plural.**

1 waiter ....
2 shop ....
3 sentence ....
4 sandwich ....

5 factory ....
6 drink ....
7 radio ....
8 house ....

9 address ....
10 party ....

2 **Put the words from Exercise 1 in the correct place in the table.**

add -s	add -es	change -y to -ies

DESCRIBING PEOPLE

's (has) got …	She's got short hair. He's got blue eyes.
's (is) / 're (are) …	They're short. Pam's young.
's (is) / are wearing	Dan's wearing a jacket and trousers. Sue and Megan are wearing hats.

Practice

3 **Complete the sentences with *is* or *has got*.**

0 Liz ...*is*.... tall and slim.
1 Jake .... wearing boots.
2 Ida .... blue eyes and brown hair.
3 Robert .... short and has got a red beard.
4 Diana .... wearing a beautiful party dress.
5 Chris .... short dark hair and a small nose.
6 Tonia .... young, slim and beautiful.

4 **Think about your family and friends and answer the questions.**

0 Who's got long brown hair?   ..Megan has got long brown hair................
1 Who's wearing black shoes today? ....
2 Who's got beautiful eyes? ....
3 Who's wearing a nice hat today? ....
4 Who's wearing blue jeans? ....
5 Who's tall and slim? ....
6 Who's wearing glasses? ....

UNIT 16

NEED, WANT

need	+ verb	+ noun
	Jo hasn't got any money. He **needs to find** work.	He **needs a job**.
want	+ verb	+ noun
	The children **want to have** an ice cream.	The children **want an ice cream**.

We always use *to* + verb after *need* and *want*.
We **need to** study more.
Julie **wants to** go to the cinema.

Practice

1 Write *need* or *want* in the correct form.

1 Oh no! My pen is broken! I .... a new one.

2 Do you .... to come to the football match with me?

3 She's eighteen next week and she .... to learn to drive a car.

4 Have you got everything for school? Do you .... anything?

5 Oh, it's very cold! I don't .... to go out today.

6 If you go on holiday to America, you .... a passport.

2 Complete the sentences with the correct form of *need* or *want* and a verb from the box.

> buy   take x2   help   come   play

0 If you're going shopping, you ..*need to take*.. some money.

1 I'm bored with this homework! I .... my computer games.

2 It's very warm today, you don't .... your jacket.

3 Ask Petra if she .... to the party.

4 I .... you but I'm busy.

5 They .... some new clothes for the party.

TOO

too + adjective = something is not right	
too hot	It's **too hot**. I need to open a window.
too expensive	She can't buy the T-shirt. It's **too expensive**.
too difficult	We can't finish the test. It's **too difficult**.

Practice

3 Complete the sentences with *too* and a word from the box.

> dirty   long   small   old
> difficult   hot   busy

0 I need some new tennis shoes. These are ..*too old*...

1 I can't do this maths problem. It's ....

2 I need to wash my T-shirt. It's ....

3 I'm sorry, I can't speak to you now. I'm ....

4 We need to drink this tea later because now it's ....

5 You're taller than me, so I can't wear your trousers. They're ....

6 Now they have a baby, they need to move house. Their flat is ....

4 Read the sentences and write the problem.

0 Oh! I can't drink this coffee!
..*It's too hot!*..

1 The temperature today is -10° C!
....

2 These shoes are great, but they cost €200!
....

3 I can't do this maths homework.
....

4 Don't use the toilet on the train!
....

5 Sarah! Don't buy that mini-skirt please!
....

UNIT 17

COMPARATIVES: SHORT AND LONG ADJECTIVES

Short adjectives			
tall	+ **-er**	+ than	Dave is **taller than** me.
safe	+ **-r**		London is **safer than** New York.
hot	double letter + **-er**		Italy is **hotter than** England.
happy	y → -i + **-er**		Liz is **happier than** her sister.
Long adjectives			
interesting	+ **more**	+ than	Maths is more **interesting than** Geography.

Practice

1 Put the words in the correct place in the table.

> fat   old   fine   angry   small   new   white   dirty
> cold   easy   hot   long   clean   sad   heavy

+ **-er**	double letter + **-er**	y → -i + **-er**	ending with -e + **-r**
taller	bigger	happier	nicer

2 Read the text and answer T (true) or F (false).

Mike and Rick are both tall. Mike is 1 metre 76 and Rick is 1 metre 80. Rick is on a diet because he weighs 95 kilos! Mike is only 75 kilos. Rick's shirts are XL (extra large); Mike's are M (medium) size. Mike is 27 years old and Rick is 29. Rick's got lots of friends – he's really nice but unfortunately Mike hasn't got many friends – he's always angry! Mike and Rick like running. Rick can run one kilometre in five minutes but Mike can do it in only four minutes.

1 Mike's taller than Rick. ....
2 Rick's fatter and bigger than Mike. ....
3 Rick's faster than Mike. ....
4 Rick's shorter than Mike. ....
5 Mike's friendlier and nicer than Rick. ....
6 Mike's older than Rick. ....
7 Rick's heavier than Mike. ....
8 Mike's slower than Rick. ....

3 Look at the information about two hotels and compare them using the words in brackets.

	€/night	number of rooms	comfort	airport	attractions
Grand Hotel	€200	100	*****	25 kms	pub, disco, fitness room, swimming pool, cabaret
Hotel Murphy	€40	30	**	2 kms	....

0 *Grand Hotel is more expensive than Hotel Murphy.* .... (expensive)
1 .... (comfortable)
2 .... (boring)
3 .... (convenient)
4 .... (peaceful)
5 .... (exciting)
6 .... (attractive)
7 .... (small)

UNIT 18

IT

We use **it**	to talk about the weather	**It's** sunny.
	as an object pronoun	That's my pen but you can use **it**.
	as a subject pronoun	I can't do this test. **It's** too difficult.

Practice

1 **Match the two parts of the sentences.**

0 It's lovely weather today. ———————
1 I can't find my phone.
2 Oh no, it's raining!
3 Look at my new camera!
4 I didn't like the new James Bond movie.
5 It's too hot in here.
6 Is that my book on the floor?

a Shall we go swimming?
b Can you open the window?
c Wow! It's fantastic!
d Really? I loved it.
e Yes, do you want it?
f It was in my bag!
g We can't play football now!

2 **Complete the dialogue with *it* or *it's*.**

Andy: Shall we go to the swimming pool? **(0)** ...It's... very hot today!
Peter: Sorry, I can't. **(1)** .... too expensive.
Andy: What about the beach then? That's cheaper.
Peter: No, I don't like the beach, **(2)** .... too dirty.
Andy: OK. Shall we go to the park and play football? **(3)** .... cool under the trees.
Peter: I don't like playing football. **(4)** .... isn't fun.
Andy: Try **(5)** .... !
Peter: No. I really don't like **(6)** ....
Andy: I give up! What do you want to do?
Peter: I don't know. **(7)** .... raining now, anyway! I've got a new DVD. Shall we watch **(8)** .... ?

PREPOSITIONS: *WITH, FOR, UNTIL*

I'm with Sue.

We're staying here for three days.

We're here until Friday.

Practice

3 **Complete the sentences with *with*, *for* and *until*.**

1 I always play volleyball .... Jackie; she's my best friend.
2 Mum! Please don't wake me up .... nine o'clock. I want to sleep!
3 We're going on holiday to Spain .... two weeks.
4 I can't help you .... I finish my homework.
5 They're going to the swimming pool. Let's go .... them!
6 Can you watch the baby .... five minutes, please?
7 My friends are staying with me .... three days.
8 We can't go swimming .... the weather is warmer.

PAST SIMPLE: *BE*

Positive (+)	Negative (–)
I / he / she / it **was**	I / he / she / it **wasn't**
We / you they **were**	We / you / they **weren't**
Questions (?)	Short answers
Was I / he / she / it?	Yes, I / he / she / it **was**. No, I / he / she / it **waasn't**.
Were we / you they?	Yes, we / you / they **were**. No, we / you / they **weren't**.

We use **was** and **were** to talk about the past.
*Sue and Bob **weren't** at home last night. They **were** at a concert.*
*I **was** late home and my dinner **was** cold. My mum **wasn't***
very happy.

Practice

1 Complete the sentences with the correct form of *was / wasn't* and *were / weren't*.

0 Were you at the concert last night? No, I ..wasn't...

1 Where .... you on Saturday night?

2 Is Meg OK? She .... at school yesterday.

3 I'm sure my homework .... on the table, but now I can't find it!

4 What .... your favourite book when you were little?

5 Mary did well in the maths test. The questions .... very difficult.

6 Your mother and I .... on holiday in Turkey in this photo.

7 Was Helen at the station the other day? Yes, she ....

8 Were your parents with you at the concert? No, they .... !

2 Complete the dialogue with *was / wasn't* and *were / weren't*.

Ann: Hi, George! Where **(1)** .... you yesterday? You **(2)** .... at school!

George: I know. I **(3)** .... in London. I **(4)** .... at a concert.

Ann: A concert! Lucky you. Who **(5)** .... the band?

George: 1D – it's my favourite band.

Ann: Great. Where **(6)** .... the concert?

George: It **(7)** .... at Wembley Stadium.

Ann: **(8)** .... they good?

George: Yes, they **(9)** .... They **(10)** .... excellent. My sister **(11)** .... really happy too!

Ann: Oh **(12)** .... she with you?

George: Yes, we **(13)** .... at the front!

Ann: **(14)** .... it a long concert?

George: Yes, it **(15)** .... about two hours. We **(16)** .... really tired at the end.

WH- QUESTIONS IN THE PRESENT AND PAST

How?	**How** are you?
What?	**What** was your first word?
What kind of?	**What kind of** music do you like?
Who?	**Who** is your best friend?
Why?	**Why** were you sad yesterday?
When?	**When** was Sarah's birthday?
Where?	**Where** were you born?

You can't answer *Wh-* questions with *Yes*, or *No*:
How is your mum?
She's fine, thanks. **Not:** ~~Yes, thanks.~~

Practice

3 Complete the questions with a question word, then match them with the replies below.

0 ..When.. were you in Manchester?

1 .... is your brother doing?

2 .... do you live?

3 .... is the boy next to Frankie?

4 .... are you wearing that strange hat?

5 .... do you finish work in the evening?

6 .... difficult was your English test?

a I was there on Tuesday 　[0]

b I live in a small town. 　[ ]

c It was easy. 　[ ]

d At 8 o'clock. 　[ ]

e He's watching TV. 　[ ]

f That's Sam. 　[ ]

g I like it! 　[ ]

UNIT 20

PAST SIMPLE

Positive (+)	Negative (–)
verb + **-ed**	**didn't** + verb
I / you / he / she / it / we / they **worked.**	I / you / he / she / it / we / they **didn't (did not)** work.

*Richard **lived** in Italy until 2013.*

*Jenny **worked** in a school.*

*We **didn't want** to go out because it was raining.*

*I **didn't walk** to school yesterday.*

Practice

1 Complete the sentences with a verb from the box in the past simple.

> travel   invite   work   want   walk   answer   live

0 I ..*travelled*.. to Greece last year on holiday.

1 Jenny .... in Japan with her mum and dad when she was a child.

2 We .... to school this morning.

3 My father .... in a bank when he was younger.

4 My sister .... to play the guitar and sing at the party last night.

5 I .... that email from my friend this morning.

6 They .... Luigi to the party, but he can't come.

2 Write the sentences in the negative form.

0 They invited my sister to the party. ...*They didn't invite my sister to the party.*.

1 Nigel and Pat liked the film. ....

2 We answered Joe's email last night. ....

3 She asked her for her phone number. ....

4 The concert started at 7.30. ....

5 The party finished very late. ....

6 The king died at the end of the story. ....

3 Complete the dialogue with the past simple form of the verbs in the box.

> invite   not want   finish   stay   walk
> ask   start   watch   not like   dance

Alison: I'm so tired.

Jackie: Really? What happened?

Alison: Well, on Monday my friend **(0)** ..*invited*.. me to a party and I
(1) .... all evening. And on Tuesday, my sister **(2)** ....
me to go to the Plaza cinema with her. I **(3)** .... the film, it
was really boring!

Jackie: And on Wednesday?

Alison: I **(4)** .... a new tennis course and the lesson **(5)** ....
.... at 9.30. By the time I **(6)** .... home, it was 10
o'clock!

Jackie: Wow! That's late!

Alison: I know! Last night I **(7)** .... to do anything! I just **(8)**
.... at home and **(9)** .... TV!

Acknowledgements

The authors would like to thank Annette Capel and Alyson Maskell for their support and guidance throughout the project.

The authors and publishers are grateful to the following for reviewing the material during the writing process:

Brazil: Catarina Kruppa; Spain: Louise Manicolo and Patricia Norris; Turkey: Çinla Sezgin.

Development of this publication has made use of the Cambridge English Corpus, a multi-billion word collection of spoken and written English. It includes the Cambridge Learner Corpus, a unique collection of candidate exam answers. Cambridge University Press has built up the Cambridge English Corpus to provide evidence about language use that helps to produce better language teaching materials.

This product is informed by English Profile, a Council of Europe-endorsed research programme that is providing detailed information about the language that learners of English know and use at each level of the Common European Framework of Reference (CEFR). For more information, please visit www.englishprofile.org

The authors and publishers acknowledge the following sources of copyright material and are grateful for the permissions granted. While every effort has been made, it has not always been possible to identify the sources of all the material used, or to trace all copyright holders. If any omissions are brought to our notice, we will be happy to include the appropriate acknowledgements on reprinting.

National Geographic Society for the adapted text on p. 114 'Interview with J Michael Fay, Conservationist' by Anne A McCormack, *National Geographic Kids*. Copyright © 1996-2013 National Geographic Society. All rights reserved.

For the sound recordings on p. 99: Track 2.32: *Beethoven - Sonata for Piano No 26 in E fl Maj Op 81a: Andante Espressivo,* artist: Premiere Classics. Copyright © Pump Audio/Getty Images/Music; *Mendelssohn - A Midsummer Night's Dream: Nocturne* artist: Premiere Classics. Copyright © Pump Audio/Getty Images/Music; *Smetana - My Fatherland (Symphonic Poem)*, artist: Premiere Classics. Copyright © Pump Audio/Getty Images/Music; *Mozart - Eine Kleine Nachtmusic, movt. 1*, artist: Charles Roland Berry. Copyright © Pump Audio/Getty Images/Music; *When Percussion Attacks 4*, artist: Silver Bullets Music Library TCB2402. Copyright © Silver Bullets/Getty Images/Music;

Track 2.33: *Children Of Hell*, artist: Silver Bullets Music Library TCB2130. Copyright © Silver Bullets/Getty Images/Music.

Photo acknowledgements

p.12 (TL): Shutterstock/wizdata, (CR): Shutterstock /Tuler Olson, (b): Shutterstock/MO_SES Premium, (c): Shutterstock/Picsfive, (d): Shutterstock/Maks Narodenko, (f): Shutterstock/maga, (h): Shutterstock/SmileStudio, (i): Shutterstock/Sergey Ash, (j): Shutterstock/Layland Masuda, (k): Shutterstock/Africa Studio; p.16 (TL): istockphoto/Juanmonino, (TC): Alamy/Ted Foxx, (TR): Alamy/dbimages, (CL): Alamy/Mitch Diamond, p.16 (C): Alamy/Tetra Images, (CR): Alamy/YAY media; p.22 (TR) & (BR): Shutterstock/Steve Buckley, (York): Alamy/eye 35, (22 CL): Shutterstock/Horia Bogdan, (C): Shutterstock/Oliver Hoffmann, (London): Shutterstock/Kamira; p.23 (BL): Alamy/David Young-Wolff, (BC): Alamy/age/footstock, (BR): Shutterstock/Gurganus Images; p.26 (TL): Shutterstock /holbox, (CL): Shutterstock /ipage, (BL): Shutterstock /Goodluz, p.32 (TL): Alamy/Mart of Images, (TR): istockphoto/Aldo Murillo, (BL): Getty Images/Fuse, (BR): Alamy/Juice images; p35 (TR): Shutterstock/Jarren Jai Wicklund; p.38: Behr & Abramson/Daniel Browning-Smith; p.44 (TR) & 45 (L): Alamy/MBI, (CR): Alamy/ Visions of America, LLC, (CL): Getty Images/Kali Nine LLC, (C): Shutterstock/artcphotos; p.45 (CR): Getty Images/Hannele Lahti, (TR): Alamy/Peter Scholey; p.46 (TL):Alamy/David Bagnal, (BR): Alamy/PCN Photography; p.48 (BL): Fotolia.com/5AM Images; p.50 (e): Alamy/Juniors Bildarchiv GmbH; p.51 (BR): Thinkstock/Creatas Images; p.54 (TL): Science Photo Library/Peter Menzel,

(TR): Alamy/Roger Bamber, (C): Science Photo Library/Alexis Rosenfeld, (BL): Getty Images/Stocktrek Images, (BR) & p.55 (TR) & (C) & p.66 (TR): Getty Images/AFP; p.55 (TL): Press Association Images/Mark Lennihan, (BR) & p.71 (B): Getty Images; p.56 (TL): Alamy/Christopher Stewart, (TR): Alamy/Valentyn Vollkov; p.57 (R): Alamy/Folio Images; p.60 (CL) & p.61 (L): Thinkstock/Leon Suharevsky, (BL): Thinkstock/Svitlana Prada, (CR): Photoshot/NHPA, (BR): Alamy/Dirk Ercken; p.61 (R): Alamy/Image Source; p.66 (B): Alamy/Bill Bachman; p.67 (BR): Alamy/AJS life; p. 70: Alamy/moodboard; p.71 (T): Getty Images/WireImage; p.76 (TR): Getty Images/Maria Toutoudak; p.79 (BL): Alamy/Mandy Godbehear; p. 80 (CR): Alamy/Garti Wyn Williams, (a): Alamy/godrick, (b): Alamy/Superstock, (c), (d) & (g) & p.120 (B): Jack Dodd, (e): Alamy/Jack Sullivan, (h): Alamy/Images of Birmingham Premium; p.82 (TL): Alamy/Yadid Levy, (CL): Corbis/Hendrik Schmidt/dpa, (C): Alamy/John Warburton-Lee Photography, (B): Thinkstock; p.86 (TR): Shutterstock/Ysbrand Cosijn; p.87 (BL): The Kobal Collection/Walt Disney Pictures, (BR): Alamy/Caro; p.88 (TL): Shutterstock/Waj, (TC): ShutterstockLuciano Mortula, (TR): Shutterstock/Justin Black, (CR): Shutterstock/Pyty, (BR): Shutterstock/Liciano Mortula, (BC): Shutterstock/Yuri Yavnik, (BL): Shutterstock/Pius Lee, (CL): Shutterstock/Art Konovalov; p.98 (B): Corbis/Carlos Garcia Rawlins/Reuters; p.102 (BL): Corbis/Patrick Ward, (BR): Alamy/Janos Csernoch; p.104 (BL): Fotolia.com/Arnelle, (BR): Alamy/Sinibomb Images, (TL): Alamy/Adrian Sherratt, (TR): Alamy/Antony Nettle; p.106 (TR): Alamy/Ellen Isaacs; p.107: Shutterstock /Brian A Jackson; p.109 (CL): Alamy/Ian Dagnall, (CR): Alamy/Finnbarr Webster, (B): Alamy/Outdoor-Archiv; p.110 (C): Alamy/Bon Appetit, (2): Alamy/Verge Images, (3): Shutterstock/Knyazevfoto.ry, (4): Shutterstock/Nordling, (5): Alamy/Vstock; p.111 (TR): Shutterstock/Flaraviere; p.112 (CL): Alamy/Photogenix; p.114 (BR): Corbis/George Steinmetz, (BL): Alamy/Marian Kaplan; p.120 (TL): The Harbour, (oil on panel), Wallis, Alfred (1855-1942) / Private Collection / Photo © Christie's Images / The Bridgeman Art Library, (TR): Sketch for 'Paris, a Rainy Day', 1877 (oil on canvas), pre-restoration (see 181504), Caillebotte, Gustave (1848-94) / Musee Marmottan Monet, Paris, France / Giraudon / The Bridgeman Art Library; p.121 (TL): M.C. Escher's "Relativity" copyright 2014 The M.C. Escher Company-The Netherlands. All rights reserved. www.mcescher.com, 121 (TR): The Bedroom, 1888 (oil on canvas), Gogh, Vincent van (1853-90) / Van Gogh Museum, Amsterdam, The Netherlands / The Bridgeman Art Library; p.123 (BL): Alamy/imagebroker.

Commissioned photography by Neil Matthews: p.10; p.14; p.24; p.34 (BR); p.36 (T); p.46 (CL); p50 (a), (b), (c), (d); p.58 (T); p59; p.68; p.80 (TR), (C); p.90 (TL), (TR), (CR); p.102 (TL), (TR), (CR); p.103 (TL); p.112 (TL), (TR), (CR), (BL), (BR);

Front cover photograph by MJTH/Shutterstock.

Illustrations

Adz (Sylvie Poggio Artists Agency) pp. 15 (Ex6, Ex8), 30, 31 (L), 39 (R), 51, 56, 62 (T), 72, 92, 95, 96, 100 (Ex2), 121 (B), 129, 144; Kathy Baxendale pp. 11 (Ex5), 12 (Ex3, Ex5), 16, 22, 23, 33 (Ex5), 35 (Ex5, Ex6 T), 43, 44, 49, 60, 76, 83 (L), 88, 106, 109 (R), 110; Francis Blake pp. 21, 100 (Ex3); Humberto Blanco (Sylvie Poggio Artists Agency) pp. 13 (Ex7), 15 (Ex9), 25, 29 (Ex4), 33 (Ex4), 34 (Ex3), 36 (BR), 39 (L), 41, 46 (B), 48, 53, 91, 103, 124, 126, 128, 139, 141 (B); Claire Bushe pp. 116-119, 123; Tom Croft pp. 46 (T), 77, 87, 99, 122; Russ Daff pp. 17, 19 (Ex5), 27, 78, 97 (L); Mark Duffin pp. 26, 34 (Ex 1), 40 (Ex1), 42, 64, 75, 83 (R), 90, 97 (TR), 98, 100 (Ex1), 111, 142; Javier Joaquin (The Organisation) pp. 10 (Ex3), 11 (Ex9), 12 (Ex2), 13 (Ex6, Ex10), 15 (Ex7), 19 (Ex8), 20, 29 (R), 31 (BR), 35 (Ex6 B), 36 (Ex1), 37, 50, 69, 79, 81, 86, 96 (Ex4), 141 (T); Garry Parsons pp. 10 (Ex2), 18, 19 (Ex7), 28, 29 (BL), 40 (B), 52, 62 (B), 74, 84, 94, 108, 109 (L), 124, 138, 154; Adam Quest pp. 58, 73.

The publishers are grateful to the following contributors: text design and layouts: emc design Ltd; cover design: Andrew Ward; picture research: Ann Thomson; audio recordings: produced by IH Sound and recorded at DSound, London; Grammar reference section: Ellen Darling, Steve Marsland and Rebecca Raynes.